EVANGEL
HOM
HINTS

A Resource for Catholic Preachers

Richard W. Chilson, C.S.P.

PAULIST PRESS
New York/Mahwah, N.J.

Art used in this book was reproduced from *Clip Art for Seasons & Celebrations of the Church Year* by Jeanne Heiberg (Paulist, 1997).

Cover design by Nick Markell

Library of Congress Cataloging-in-Publication Data

Chilson, Richard.
Evangelization homily hints : a resource for Catholic preachers / Richard W. Chilson.
p. cm.
ISBN 0-8091-3932-4 (alk. paper)
1. Evangelistic work. 2. Lectionary preaching—Catholic Church. I. Title.
BX2347.4.C485 2000
251—dc21

99-058997
CIP

Published by Paulist Press
997 Macarthur Boulevard
Mahwah, New Jersey 07430

www.paulistpress.com

Printed and bound in the
United States of America

Contents

To Ken McGuire, C.S.P.,
who coaxed this book from me
over the years,

and to the people of Guest House,
who coaxed me
back to life

in gratitude

Introduction

Beginning with the Church's turn toward viewing the world not as opponent but as fellow pilgrim as a result of the Second Vatican Council, continuing with Pope Paul VI's *Evangelii Nuntiandum,* gathering force with continued encyclicals of John Paul II and the American bishops' letters such as *Go and Make Disciples,* the church has at the official level embraced evangelization wholeheartedly. The hierarchy has clarified the themes of evangelization, and the bishops' letters have begun to unite these themes with strategies appropriate to our American culture. But the ultimate ministry of evangelization lies with all Catholics—not just the ordained.

American Catholics have been inundated with programs over the past twenty years. When anything new arises in Catholic consciousness, we develop another program to achieve our goals. So, when pastoral ministers now hear that we must be aware of evangelization, we are likely to feel overwhelmed. Not another program!

And you are right. We do not need another program for evangelization. As we have learned over the past twenty years with the Rite of Christian Initiation of Adults (RCIA), the catechumenate is not another program. It is an essential component of any Christian community. And its presence transforms the entire community.

Without it a church lacks an essential dimension. A catechumenate clarifies and focuses our understanding of church as a place of continuous conversion; new Christians renew our community with their gifts and stories. We find a central vision for our catechesis. Small communities of faith point a way to be church in the midst of the mega-church.

So evangelization also demands not a program but a vision. It needs to become an essential and crucial part of our core Christian experience. Every baptized person is baptized not only for him or herself but for others. We are to become the gospel we have heard and experienced so that others through us may share the source of our joy.

We need to think of evangelization as a necessary component of every ministry from greeters, to schools, even to bingo games. For the evangelizing vision to take route in our Christian life we need to adopt this viewpoint for every area of our life as a parish and as Christians.

The first goal of evangelization as outlined by the American bishops is to evangelize the faithful. Each and every Christian is throughout his or her life called to a deeper and deeper conversion to the gospel. We may be able to point to a date on which we were converted for the first time. But there is no date on which that conversion is concluded short of death. If our conversion is not ongoing, we are in effect spiritually dead.

Who are the first people to whom we are sent to bring the gospel? Our fellow Catholics. And each of us here is both evangelizer and evangelized. This is not a task for ministers alone. Who evangelizes the clergy? The laity. As we share our faith stories with one another, have we not experienced a deeper dimension of the gospel hearing it from another person's perspective and history?

Naturally the minister has a more structured role within the church and within the evangelization ministry. It is the minister's job to keep the vision alive for the community. And this happens primarily through preaching: the reason for this book.

Some communities have set aside one Sunday a month to focus on evangelization. While this may be one way to begin, it also misses the point. Evangelization is not something special we do. It is a crucial part of who we are. While it may be beneficial to heighten consciousness about evangelization with a special homily each month, the ideal would be to allow the evangelizing vision to permeate every homily. Not every homily would be about evangelization, but the perspective would inform each homily.

This book does not provide evangelization homilies for the lectionary. Rather it offers suggestions to teach and encourage reading the scriptures with an eye to their evangelical scope. Often it simply asks questions the scriptures raise when read from an evangelistic outlook. It provides ideas and ways you can begin transforming your parish into an evangelizing community.

At present we still grope with the whole vocabulary of evangelization. The word elicits from many Catholics visions of going door to door, asking whether you are saved. Most Catholics feel uncomfortable with such tactics. And rightfully so, for there is a Catholic style and flavor to evangelization. But it will take time for us to learn and practice this new way. The hints in this book will help the preacher begin to articulate this Catholic understanding of evangelization. It provides the first steps in learning this new language.

It will take time (and time as the church sees it, not as Americans see it) for this vision to permeate our faith. There is no quick fix. So proceed slowly. Test things. Evaluate. Share ideas within the parish and with other communities. Slowly you will come to see the faith through the eyes of evangelization. It will become a crucial dimension of who we are as Catholics. Gone will be the day when people will think that you have to be born a Catholic in order to be really Catholic. We will be changed, and so will people and even cultures.

For although the first goal of evangelization is our own selves and our communities, there are two other goals as well. Good news has been entrusted to us. How do we reach out in welcome to those who do not have faith? There are more non-believers in this country than people of faith. (By "people of faith," I do not limit myself to Catholics or even to Christians, but include those who embrace other religions as well.) Most of our neighbors do not have a spiritual vision by which they understand and live their lives. We have a great treasure. The church is asking us to find ways and means to share that treasure with others.

We search for ways to enable people of no faith to hear the good news of Jesus. The gospel is not unchanging. Yes, Jesus Christ is the same yesterday, today, and tomorrow. But the actual words, ideas, and media we employ to communicate this gospel must change with the times and the culture. How can we tell our story of faith in such a way that a twentieth-century American can come to accept its truth? To do so, we have to speak in the context of modern science, psychology, and communications.

A second group consists of our brothers and sisters who no longer actively practice the faith. Inactive Catholics form the second largest religious group in the United States today. Yes, they have heard the gospel. But they have heard it in fragments or distorted, so that it did not bring them life. They may have been wounded by the church. Perhaps they simply drifted away and are just waiting for a simple invitation to come home. Whatever the reason, we need to go in search of them so that they too might hear again or for the first time the freeing power of the gospel. It is up to us to take the initiative to welcome them back into their family of faith. Do we care that they are not with us? How can we manifest our concern for our brothers and sisters?

With other Christians, we share a common faith. In dialogue with them, we all grow through a deeper encounter with Jesus Christ. With other religions, by sharing experiences such as the way we pray we all deepen our own understandings of God.

Catholics are greatly indebted to the scripture scholarship developed by Protestants in the last century. Many Catholics have rediscovered our own contemplative tradition by learning to meditate from Buddhists. And we in turn may have helped to spur the new phenomenon of socially engaged Buddhism emerging out of Buddhism's encounter with the West. All of this is evangelization. It is not proselytizing. We are not out to convert the other, although that may happen. We are sharing with one another while we continue on our own paths our common pilgrimage toward God.

The third goal of evangelization outlined by the bishops is American culture. How can the saving word touch and transform our common life as Americans? Here we encounter enormous issues such as peace and justice, the sanctity of human life, the fate of the poor, and concern for the environment. What does the gospel say to these concerns? How can economics be leavened by gospel compassion?

But in addition to such global problems there are thousands of other, small-scale ways we can make a difference in our society. How can we contribute to the building of neighborhood and community? How do we care for the poor and victims of injustice? How do we reach out to the wounded? How do we address issues of violence and abuse in our own community? All these people and situations need to hear good news. Our social action ministries can proclaim good news in ways that touch and transform our culture. As we allow the evangelizing vision to shape our own appreciation of the gospel message, we will come to see that to reach out to others with kindness and hope as we have been reached out to is essential to following Jesus.

Suggestions for Using This Book

Obviously this book is most useful to parish preachers. Without preaching that evangelizes, the parish has little chance of implementing evangelization. Since evangelization is such a new concept for Catholics, it will take many different presentations for us to begin thinking with an evangelizing mindset. While you do not want to make every single homily focus upon evangelization, ask yourself whether there is an evangelizing dimension to each homily. The material here is geared to provide stimulation for your thinking along these lines. There is no way to speak abstractly about evangelization. How you preach depends upon your local community and environs.

This book would also be useful to the parish liturgical committee as well as the liturgist. How can we begin to think of liturgy as evangelization? How do we make the liturgy more inviting, and how emphasize the sending forth? Do the songs and music we choose promote our mission? Do we look at the roles of the various liturgical ministers as being evangelistic? For example, are there greeters each Sunday to welcome people? Is someone in charge of a program for welcoming newcomers?

Most parishes begin the ministry of evangelization by setting up a committee. This group should familiarize itself with the key documents from Rome, the American Conference of Bishops, as well as the local diocese. The homily hints will inspire them to discover ways they can implement evangelization on the local scene.

Some parishes will choose to place the homily hints in the parish bulletin. You will probably want to choose just a few sentences to stimulate thought and discussion. You might put the notes in the bulletin a week ahead so that on the following Sunday many will have thought about the readings along with the preacher. Then you might invite those interested to remain afterward for a brief discussion.

Although evangelization may begin with a special task force or committee, it must permeate the entire parish structure. This book could serve as a resource for the parish council and other committees as it provides help for viewing ministry through evangelizing eyes.

Finally, although the Rite of Christian Initiation of Adults is part of the overall evangelization ministry, evangelization should inform the catechesis. We want to give birth to new Christians who see themselves as signs of good news for others. This book helps RCIA directors bring an evangelizing dimension to the Sunday Service of the Word dismissal group.

1

Season of Advent

First Sunday of Advent

CYCLE A

Isaiah 2:1–5 The Lord will gather all nations in eternal peace to form the kingdom of God.

Romans 13:11–14 The time has come, our salvation is near.

Matthew 24:37–44 Stay awake, you must be ready.

Advent is a season of wakefulness, which both the second reading and the gospel stress. The time is at hand. Wake up! We have a tendency to fall into complacency unless a crisis jolts us. Advent reminds us of the crisis that looms over us: this world is passing away to make way for the kingdom of God. We live in a time of ecological crisis, although many people still do not realize its import. We are destroying and ruining God's creation. Part of our mission rests in awakening our brothers and sisters to the present moment so that we can take action while there is still time.

Isaiah speaks of the day when all the nations will be drawn to the Lord's mountain. Healing misunderstandings and misperceptions between peoples falls to evangelization. What is our church doing to heal the racial tensions present in our society? Are we seen as a church open to all people, or do we seem like a church of the select few? What can we do to reach out and bring all people together in our shared humanity as beloved creatures of God?

CYCLE B

Isaiah 63:16–17, 19; 64:2–7 Oh, that you would tear the heavens apart and come down.

1 Corinthians 1:3–9 The revelation we looked for, Christ Jesus our Lord.

Mark 13:33–37 Stay awake! You never know when the Lord will come.

Keeping vigilant is a primary Advent theme and is certainly relevant to the ministry of evangelization. As bearers of the good news, we need to be constantly on watch for the opportunity to share the gospel. When is a person, group, or society open to hearing the good news? When do they invite us by a question or a concern to share our faith with them? Whenever this opportunity arises we must be ready. It may seem like a casual question: How do you keep your head in the Christmas rush? At that time we must be ready to say something about Advent: how it is a time of quiet, waiting, treasuring the person at the center of all the activity—the Prince of Peace whose coming in glory we await with eagerness and expectation. To be able to share such a message we must be living it. All our evangelization, if it is to be genuine must come out of our lived experience. What are we doing this Advent to keep watch for the Lord? How are we preparing not just for the Christmas holidays but for the Lord's coming into our lives?

CYCLE C

Jeremiah 33:14–16 I will cause a good seed to spring forth from David.

1 Thessalonians 3:12–4:2 When Christ comes may he strengthen your hearts in holiness.

Luke 21:25–28, 34–36 Your redemption is near at hand.

Our evangelization theme today focuses upon the second reading. Paul asks that the Lord may increase our love for one another and for all. Evangelization is not something we can separate off into a special ministry. It is intrinsically connected to our experience of the gospel and of life in Christ. It begins with God's love and care for us, which we must experience in order to come to know God at all. This love and care we may find through another person or through the Christian community.

Pastoral care is an essential component of the catechumenate, whose ministry is first of all to show inquirers the hospitality of Jesus. Jesus spent much of his own ministry eating with people (usually the wrong kind in the eyes of the respectable leaders of his day). He made those who were alienated feel welcome. He invited himself to Zacchaeus the tax collector's house when no one else would have gone there.

As we begin the year, let us consider the many ways in which God has shown love for us. How does our community reflect this love? How do we welcome the stranger and make him or her feel at home? How do we reach out in love to those in trouble in our neighborhood?

Second Sunday of Advent

CYCLE A

Isaiah 11:1–10 He judges the poor with justice.

Romans15:4–9 Christ, the hope of all men.

Matthew 3:1–12 Repent, for the kingdom of heaven is close at hand.

Both Isaiah and Paul envision peace and harmony springing up on the Day of the Lord. We are called to be signs and bearers of peace in our world. As Pope Paul VI taught, peace is to be understood as development, not as the status quo or stagnation.

How do we assist in the development of peoples and of the Earth? Does our parish engage in efforts to help the homeless and the poor claim their rightful place with all others in God's Kingdom? How do we promote peace and harmony within our own community? How do we handle tensions between different groups within the parish? Do we acknowledge the strains and seek methods to reach consensus? Or do we pretend they are not there and hope they will go away?

Peace and harmony are not only gifts we are promised. They can be ours today, but only if we stir ourselves from our present situation in order to deal honestly and respectfully with others. If we are a sign of harmony in our community, we are performing our mission to proclaim the gospel.

CYCLE B

Isaiah 40:1–5, 9–11 Make straight in the desert the way of the Lord.

2 Peter 3:8–14 We wait for new heavens and a new earth.

Mark 1:1–8 Prepare a way for the Lord.

Peter speaks of God's generous patience with us and with all creation. We are living in the time of that great patience. While some are eager to proclaim the end of the world, that would be premature at best. We do not know the time. In the coming years more and more voices will be raised, using Peter's words in the second half of the reading, which threaten the end of everything. Our message of evangelization might better use the substance of the first half.

We are living in the time of God's generous patience. How has God been patient with you? How long has God given you to begin to see the light? Testimonies about God's patience are very inviting. Saint Augustine's hymn is one of the best known: "Late have I loved thee, beauty most rare. I sought thee without and thou wert all along within." Although the end time may be an occasion of panic, we need not fuel that fire. We still live in the time of God's patience: a powerful testimony to God's infinite love for creation.

CYCLE C

Baruch 5:1–9 Jerusalem—God will show your splendor.

Philippians 1:4–6, 8–11 Show yourselves sinless and without blame in the day of Christ.

Luke 3:1–6 All mankind shall see the salvation of God.

The Baptist in today's gospel tells us to prepare the way of the Lord. Before people can hear the gospel or good news, they must be put in a state of mind that makes them receptive to this. Before we can hear the gospel as the good news that it is, we need to be made aware of just how bad things are. It is easy for people to complain about the state of things, and some Christians seem to delight in lamenting that everything is going to hell in a handbasket.

But the truth is that this world is in need of a savior. We need to wake up. And today more than ever the message of the Baptist may be welcomed if we proclaim it correctly. John begins not with a list of sins, but with a wake-up call. Something good is coming. Prepare to receive the Lord, who will transform our world. We have in the gospel a message that God's transformative power is in our lives and our world now. Some today are tempted to give up hope. Christians can never do that, because we know that God is preparing a wonderful thing for all creation. This is the message we carry today to people who may feel overwhelmed by the present situation. Do not despair! Our Lord is coming with salvation. Let us prepare to receive him.

Certain things in our world may tempt us to throw up our hands in resignation. We are on the verge of ruining our environment not just for our grandchildren but for ourselves. New viruses resistant to our best drugs are spawning. Respect for life in all forms seems to be dwindling.

Rather than wring our hands at these and similar problems we Christians are called to bring the spark of hope. God has not abandoned us and will never do so. We look not to the past but to the future coming of Christ. A new hope is given to us this and every Advent—not about someone who came centuries ago, but about a God who in love is coming to be with us now in this time and in these crises. With such a hope we can move out of paralysis and begin to address these great crises and with God's help resolve them.

Third Sunday of Advent

CYCLE A

Isaiah 35:1–6, 10 God himself will come and save us.

James 5:7–10 You also must be patient; do not lose heart, the Lord's coming will be soon.

Matthew 11:2–11 Are you the one who is to come, or shall we wait for someone else?

All three readings share the theme of waiting for the Lord's coming. Christians also await the coming of

God's kingdom and the second coming of Christ. As we approach the millennium, the air is filled with ideas about the end of the world. Many Christians encourage focusing upon the end and meditate constantly upon the awful judgment that God will render.

However, more important than the idea of judgment is the hope that lies in each of these readings. In the gospel, the imprisoned John the Baptist hopes that the one he foretold has come. James encourages his congregation to be patient in waiting for the Lord's Day. Isaiah sees the future blossoming of the desert and entreats courage for the fainthearted and strength for the weak.

As the air fills with cries of hopelessness and despair about our future, we have a mission to bring hope. Creation and history are still in God's hands; let us have hope in the new thing God is bringing into our world. We can calm those who are fearful or despairing. We might bring strength to those who are weak. The Day of the Lord we await does involve a judgment when the wheat is separated from the chaff, but it also brings about a new age when God will gather up all creation in peace and harmony. We Catholics might sustain this great hope amidst those fearful of the end of time.

CYCLE B

Isaiah 61:1–2, 10–11 I exult for joy in the Lord.

1 Thessalonians 5:16–24 May you all be kept blameless, spirit, soul and body, for the coming of our Lord Jesus Christ.

John 1:6–8, 19–28 There stands among you, unknown to you, the one who is coming after me.

John the Baptist is a model evangelizer. He knows he is but a finger pointing at the sun. He himself is not the sun, although whatever light is in him comes from the sun. So it is with us. We are filled with light—our church, our community, ourselves. God wants us to let that light be seen by others so that they too might come to live in the light. But we ourselves—neither as individuals, nor as a church—are the light. We are but witnesses to the light who is Christ ever coming everywhere and in everyone who comes into the world. He is the one and the only one to whom we should point. And all our lives and ministry, like John's, are a preparation for the shining of that light ever more fully.

The second reading tells us how we are to witness: through our rejoicing. Rejoice always! The word resounds through the first two readings as well as the psalm. Catholics used to call this "Gaudete" or "Rejoice!" Sunday. We are not to be heralds of gloom and doom. We rejoice because we await God's coming in glory. Our message as well as our lives should be one of rejoicing. After all it is good news we are called to share.

CYCLE C

Zephaniah 3:14–18 The Lord will exult you. He will renew you by his love.

Philippians 4:4–7 The Lord is near.

Luke 3:10–18 What, then must we do?

Let us continue to focus upon the Baptist. Last week he called us to prepare for the Lord's coming. This week he shows us just how to prepare. He does not call us to anything heroic. Rather he asks us to live honestly as who we are. Do your job well. Do not let power go to your head. Be content with what you have and what you are doing. Do not be tempted to abuse your place and power.

It is a message of incredible common sense. Yet it is

a message we and our society need to hear. How might the Baptist's injunctions apply to America today? To our particular community? How can our parish go about sharing its surplus with others who do not have enough? Might we make a gift each week of a share of our collection to help out those in need? Such a gift announced at the start of the prayer of the faithful would tell everyone in the congregation that here is a community that shares its surplus of coats with those who have none.

Fourth Sunday of Advent

CYCLE A

Isaiah 7:10–14 The virgin shall conceive.

Romans1:1–7 Jesus Christ, a descendant of David, is the Son of God.

Matthew 1:18–24 Jesus was born of Mary who was betrothed to Joseph, a relative of David.

Jesus is the ultimate sign, the core of the good news we proclaim as Christians. The readings today witness to this historical individual as the embodiment of our hopes and desires. In Isaiah, God provides Ahaz with a sign that God is with Israel. The king requires such a sign because he is afraid to act as God has asked him to behave. He is told that a young woman will give birth. Let that be a sign that you can trust in God.

The young woman in question was not originally the Virgin Mary, but a young woman in Ahab's court. Yet when Matthew went searching the scriptures in order to deepen his community's understanding of Jesus, he found this passage of Isaiah foretelling Jesus' own birth of a virgin. Matthew's concern was to anchor Jesus in the

Israelite tradition, to show how he was the answer to all of Israel's hopes and prayers.

How can Jesus be the answer for the longings of our own day and time? What does he have to give to modern Americans? As Matthew shows how Jesus fulfills the dreams of Israel, so in our proclamation of the good news we must disclose how Jesus and his message offer hope, healing, comfort, and guidance to modern Americans.

We would best realize this task by asking how he makes our own life fuller. What difference does Jesus make for me? For my family? For my church? Now let us, like Matthew, share this good news with our friends and neighbors.

CYCLE B

2 Samuel 7:1–5, 8–11, 16 The Lord will make the house of David secure forever.

Romans 16:25–27 The mystery kept secret for endless ages is now made clear.

Luke 1:26–38 You shall conceive and bear a son.

Paul speaks of the mystery hidden through the ages and now revealed. That mystery is not some secret knowledge or technique. No, we see it clearly in today's gospel. It is the mystery of love that wishes to come and dwell among us. The first reading speaks of God taking up residence in a temple. But in truth God comes to a simple young maiden and courts us by becoming one of us.

This mystery is not something that only happened long ago. God continues to take up residence in each of us if we only, like Mary, say, "Yes." How God is living and working in our life is the essence of the good news we bear. Sure we can tell the old scripture stories. But God is writing a scripture in our lives today. This contemporary scripture, which tells how God is finding a home with us today, requires only a listening heart to be understood. No scripture studies; no degree in theology needed. That was the mystery Paul possessed—how God had touched and befriended him. That was the mystery Mary proclaimed. That same mystery with a different cast of characters—us—is the gospel we are sent to announce.

CYCLE C

Micah 5:1–4 Out of you will be born the one who is to rule over Israel.

Hebrews 10:5–10 I am coming to do your will.

Luke 1:39–45 Why should it happen that I am honored with a visit from the mother of my Lord?

The prophet Micah in today's first reading speaks of Bethlehem, a small insignificant town of Israel, as chosen to give birth to the Messiah. Indeed Micah himself is not a very significant prophet for Christians. This passage is the only time Micah appears in the three-year Sunday lectionary. Yet most Christians honor him and recognize him for this passage alone.

So it can be with us. We do not have to shoulder the immense burden of God's work alone. We are each gifted by God. God, if we allow it, will use our gifts to further God's work. What is it we are gifted with? How do we see the good news of Jesus working out in our lives? How can we like Micah proclaim this good news?

If we think of evangelization as bringing the good news to the whole world, we can easily be overwhelmed and lapse into resignation. But if we can ask what little part we have to contribute to the overall effort, as individuals, as parish community, we, like Micah, will find our place in the company of the prophets. How have you personally experienced the good news? How have we as a parish community, through what has happened to us, come to see the gospel taking flesh here today? Let us like Mary rush out to tell our kinsfolk what so fills us with joy.

2

Season of Christmas

December 25—Christmas—
Cycles A, B, and C

Isaiah 62:11–12 Your savior is born.

Titus 3:4–7 His own compassion saved us.

Luke 2:15–20 The shepherds found Mary and Joseph, and the baby lying in the manger.

Although it might seem that Christmas is not a time to focus on evangelization, let us reconsider. Christmas is a time when many non-Catholics and former Catholics attend services. Our churches are full of people whom we may not see again until Ash Wednesday or Easter. What a perfect opportunity to welcome them and show how we would like to provide a home for them.

The story today is of a child born in a stable because there was no room at the inn. Some people might perceive our church as such an inn, with no room for them. Yet the very word Catholic means "universal." We are the church James Joyce wonderfully described as, "Here comes everybody." In this church, no one should be excluded. No need to be a saint. We are a community of sinners; because of this child we are confident that God loves us and will stay with us no matter how far we stray. Here is a place to come when you have been turned out elsewhere. Here is a home for the poor shepherds to whom the glad tidings were first proclaimed. Shepherds were the outcasts of their own day. Here is a home as well for kings to do homage. This child, so poor he had no proper birthplace, will find a home in whatever poor stable, in whatever humble heart will make room for him.

Sunday in the Octave of Christmas —Feast of the Holy Family

Sirach 3:2–6,12–14 He who fears the Lord honors his parents.

Colossians 3:12–21 Concerning the Christian life in the world.

A: Matthew 2:13–15,19–23 Take the child and his mother and flee into Egypt.

B: Luke 2:22–40 The child grew to maturity, and he was filled with wisdom.

C: Luke 2:41–42 His parents found him in the temple, sitting among doctors, listening to them

Jesus is born into a specific family. His experience within that family helped him mature and grow in his knowledge and intimacy of God and God's love. In the family, all human beings first meet with acceptance, nurture, education, and we hope a knowledge of God. Today the family seems to be falling apart in our country. Yet without a nurturing environment for children, it is impossible for them to grow up into healthy adults.

Let us look at how we might encourage and foster family life within our parish and community. Do we offer help to families in trouble either financially or emotionally? Is marriage enrichment a central part of our parish life, and do we invite the larger community of married people to join us in such workshops? How can we help link families to one another? Families with newborns go through certain common crises and challenges. They often come to us for baptism. How might our community offer them continued community and support as they begin to raise their children?

The same is true for parents of teenagers—a very difficult rite of passage both for the teens and their families. How can our parish community resources and a supportive community and environment enable teens to pass through these exciting and difficult years? And how can we help the parents of teenagers share their experiences, their struggles, and their successes with one another? Lots of people are talking about building and supporting the family. What can our church actually do to help families? We can start by asking our own family members what they seek and need for their strength and growth.

January 1—Solemnity of Mary of God—Cycles A, B, and C

Numbers 6:22–27 They will call down my name on the children of Israel and I will bless them.

Galatians 4:4–7 When his appointed time came, God sent his Son, born of a woman.

Luke 2:16–21 The shepherds found Mary and Joseph, and the infant lying in a crib....When the eighth day came they gave him the name of Jesus.

The blessing from Numbers has become a favorite of both Jews and Christians, but rather than limit ourselves to this particular blessing, let us consider the idea of blessing itself. Scripture is filled with blessings. We give thanks to God for the blessings bestowed upon us. A new priest's first blessing is eagerly sought by all. Our church offers a huge book of blessings for all occasions. We are called to mediate God's blessings to one another and to our world.

Blessing is a work of evangelization: of announcing the good news in our midst. The most important thing an older man can do for a young man is bless him. How much of the crisis in our society among youth is due to the absence of such blessing? Do we make it a point to bless our children and youth? Or do we speak only to criticize?

It is a commonly known fact that critical mail outweighs mail bearing good news. The critics are more likely to write to Congress or to Rome than those who think well of what is happening. Let us take it upon ourselves this new year to engage in the work of blessing. Let us bless our children, our ministers, our public servants. Blessing brings God's abundance and peace. We are a people of blessing. Let us show ourselves to our community and to our world as such. Are there people or groups in our community whom we can hold up and bless as a Church? Let us do so.

Sunday after New Year's—Epiphany of the Lord—Cycles A, B, and C

Isaiah 60:1–6 The glory of the Lord shines upon you.

Ephesians 3:2–3, 5–6 The revelation means that pagans now share the same inheritance, that they are parts of the same body.

Matthew 2:1–12 We have come from the East to worship the king.

The feast of Epiphany is all about evangelization: God announces the good news of the Savior to all peoples. Isaiah speaks of a day when peoples and nations shall be gathered in unity around the light. Any evangelization effort must promote understanding among peoples in the hope of furthering the coming together in harmony of different cultures. Part of the joy of being a Roman Catholic is the rich diversity within our church. We are not a church of one language, class, or ethnicity, but of all peoples. In many parishes, the image of Isaiah is enacted when the community goes forward to communion. Then we see the incredible richness which we share—all races, all classes are gathering around the light of the Eucharist, which feeds us and enlightens our way.

The star the wise men followed was also a light announcing the coming of Christ to all the world. It was in the sky for everyone to see, but only these wise men saw it and followed it in the hope they might find the king. They were not Jews, and yet they knew of this king's coming from their own traditions and wisdom. And every religion hopes for a day of unity when all are gathered to the light. Jesus is the one in whom that light shines forth most strongly. How might we permit his light to shine through us without being obscured by our own ideas and prejudices of what that light means? And we are called to search out his light already shining in other cultures. Finding the light there helps people of those cultures recognize the same light in Jesus and helps us to allow that light to shine more clearly in our own tradition.

Sunday after Epiphany—Baptism of the Lord—Cycles A, B, and C

Isaiah 42:1–4, 6–7 Here is my servant, my chosen one in whom my soul delights.

Acts of the Apostles 10:34–38 God anointed him with the Holy Spirit and with power.

Matthew 3:13–17 When Jesus was baptized the heavens were opened and the Spirit of God came upon him.

Like John the Baptist, our ministry is to point to the Christ. Whatever we accomplish, like John, we need to acknowledge that it is not done out of our power or ability but by the grace of Christ working through us.

As we grow in the knowledge of Christ we grow in wisdom. So in the second reading Peter comes to the realization that God shows no partiality. There really is no division among people, between those who are chosen and those who are not. Jew and Gentile no longer make sense to Peter. And he arrives at this wisdom through his experience of Jesus and what Jesus stands for.

The life of an evangelist is one of continuing growth. God accepts us as we are, but that does not mean that we must not allow the wisdom of God to change and transform us. As we come to know more kinds of people, we also must come to the realization, like Peter, that God does not play favorites. All people are gifted and beloved by God. No one is left out. And our message should enable each and every person to hear that indeed they are loved and cherished. The proof of this love of God is in the person of Jesus, his beloved Son, who in turn gives his life out of love for us.

February 2—Presentation of the Lord—Cycles A, B, and C

Malachi 3:1–4 The Lord whom you seek will come to the temple.

Hebrews 2:14–18 He had to be made like his fellows in all things.

Luke 2:22–40 My eyes have seen your saving power.

This feast is a festival of light. Traditionally, candles used throughout the year are blessed today. Simeon hails Jesus as the light coming into the world to guide the Gentiles and give glory to Israel. Jesus is our light. He is the light that reveals the way. He is the light we wish to share with others through evangelization.

In what ways does Jesus provide light for our lives? How does reading the scripture provide light for your day? How do the Church's teachings illumine you? How is our community enlightened by Jesus?

Many people are, like Simeon, waiting for this light. They long for it, thirst for it. We need to do what Mary and Joseph did today. We need to bring Jesus to these people so that they may see for themselves that he is the light. No one needs to convince Simeon once he has seen the child. Jesus himself will convince those he meets. But he needs us to bring him to people, as Mary and Joseph brought him to Simeon.

They brought Jesus to the temple. We in turn must bring Jesus to our church. She will bless Jesus, but she will in turn be enlightened by him. Through our own experiences of the light, the church grows in wisdom. She comes to see the countless ways in which Jesus illumines the world and the strength of the light within her grows. Evangelization is never simply a movement outward to non-Christians. It must always also include movement inward, to the center of the church herself, so that she might bless the light and be better illumined by it. The saints' experience of the light has often taught and corrected the church so that her own understanding of Jesus grows.

3

Season of Lent

First Sunday of Lent

CYCLE A

Genesis 2:7–9; 3:1–7 Creation of our first parents, and sin.

Romans 5:12–19 The results of the gift, Jesus Christ, outweigh one person's sin.

Matthew 4:1–11 Jesus fasted for forty days and nights.

The story of Jesus' temptation in the wilderness provides three models to imitate in our desire to be bearers of the good news. Matthew sets up the story as a reflection upon Israel's forty-year sojourn in the desert. While Israel fell into temptation, Jesus as the new Israel shows how God's people should act. By refusing to turn the stones into bread, Jesus denies himself and opens himself to God. We live in a consumer society. Do we buy into it? Do we let material possessions dominate our lives? How can we witness to values that transcend consumerism?

Second, Jesus refuses to put God to the test. We may pray for various things, and there is nothing wrong with this. But do we accept ourselves and our lives as God has given them to us? Are we continually complaining and asking that things be different? Or do we show an acceptance of life and an acquiescence to God's will for us?

Finally, there is a temptation to power. This world runs on power. Whoever has power has control. People will do almost anything to get and hold onto power. Jesus refuses this temptation. For him all power resides with God. What is our attitude toward power as individuals and as a community? Are we concerned about prestige and what we can gain? Or do we seek to serve one another and our neighbors? During this Lent, let us as individuals and as a community move closer to the lifestyle of Jesus in today's gospel. We too are the new Israel; let us show that image to the world.

CYCLE B

Genesis 9:8–15 I will recall the covenant between myself and you....The waters shall never again become a flood to destroy all flesh.

1 Peter 3:18–22 The water of the flood is a type of the baptism which saves you now.

Mark 1:12–15 He was tempted by Satan, and the angels looked after him.

Peter tells us that Christ died for our sins so that he might lead us toward God. Jesus as the way to God is a major metaphor. You might say that the reason we carry the crucifix in procession and place it at the front of our churches symbolizes Jesus crucified as the one who continues to lead us toward God. As we begin this Lenten journey, when we seek to follow the crucified one even more closely, let us ask ourselves as individuals and as a community how we might allow Jesus to lead us today.

Peter, along with the first reading, reminds us of the covenant with Noah. God's mercy saved Noah and his children from the flood. We too are a people saved from all types of floods and disasters. The story of our salvation from our personal floods is crucial to our ministry of evangelization.

The story of Jesus comes alive when it is heard in the context of our own story. How has our parish community experienced the saving power of God? How have each one of us experienced the salvation of God in our life? Telling this story is uttering the gospel anew. In the story resides the power of God to lead people toward him.

CYCLE C

Deuteronomy 26:4–10 The confession of faith of the elect.

Romans 10:8–13 The confession of faith of the believers in Christ.

Luke 4:1–13 Filled with the Holy Spirit, Jesus was led by the Spirit through the wilderness where he was tempted.

Today we officially enter the Lenten season, and the gospel speaks of Jesus going off into the wilderness. If we look at Jesus' ministry, we see that he follows a pattern of going into the world and then withdrawing for prayer and reflection. Today's gospel follows Jesus' baptism. There he has heard the call from God, and he comes to understand himself as the beloved Son. Rather than rush out into ministry from this event, he withdraws to the desert where in prayer and fasting he might come to a deeper appreciation of who he is and what his mission is to be. The temptations Luke describes help Jesus to delineate himself and his work.

If we are to enter into Jesus' ministry, we too must follow his method. We cannot always be on the front lines. We cannot always be doing. During Lent, the entire church joins her Lord in the wilderness, so that together we might discern what we are called to do.

Our particular community is committed to evangelization: proclaiming the good news. But during this Lenten season, we too might withdraw in prayer. We ask to be shown the next step. We ask that our vocation be tested. We ask for the guidance of the Holy Spirit.

Ministry is a going back and forth from work to prayer. Work alone is not enough. We must constantly bring our work to God in prayer and seek to discern God's will for us. Like Jesus, this Lent let us ask ourselves individually and as a community, Who are we? and, What is God calling us to do to proclaim the gospel?

Second Sunday of Lent

CYCLE A

Genesis 12:1–4 The call of Abraham, the father of God's people.

2 Timothy 1:8–10 God has saved us and called us to be holy.

Matthew 17:1–9 His face shone like the sun.

The first two readings speak of God's call, first to Abraham and then to us. This summons pulls us out of our normal routine. Indeed, it drew Abraham away from his native land and all with which he and Sarah were familiar. And while the call may not affect us to the extent that it influenced Abraham and Sarah, it also summons us to a new life.

Paul says we have been given the gift of salvation not because we deserved it or because of anything we have done. Our call is a mystery known only to God. But because of it we experience life more fully. We know the Lord and we know of our redemption. And we are called not merely to experience this redemption but to shine the good news forth to others. In the gospel, Jesus on the mountain allows the three disciples to witness the dazzling glory of God. He shines forth with the light. We too, like those disciples, have seen that light in some way in our lives. Because we have seen the light, we in turn are commissioned to allow that same light to shine through us so that others may come to know the glory we have experienced.

CYCLE B

Genesis 22:1–2, 9, 10–13, 15–18 The sacrifice of Abraham, our father in faith.

Romans 8:31–34 God did not spare his own Son.

Mark 9:2–10 This is my Son, the beloved, listen to him.

Whose side is God on? Paul is absolutely convinced: God is with us. And if so, who or what can possibly be against us? Certainly things do not always go easily for Christians. We suffer sickness, misunderstanding, and oppression just like everyone else. But to know in the midst of whatever troubles we are undergoing that the Creator of the universe is on our side, is deeply committed to us and our cause, should help us through our difficulty. Christians have no cause but to be supremely optimistic. There is no real contest between God and any force we might imagine is opposed to God, whether a disease, some worldly power, or some form of tyranny. Although we may be misunderstood, ridiculed, or even persecuted by forces in this world, we know that in God's eyes we are beloved sons and daughters.

This is a powerful message we have to carry to people who are oppressed or shut out of this world and its affairs. This is a message of tremendous inclusion—God embracing all in love and God's promise to vindicate all who stand with Jesus. For centuries Christians have said that the heart of Paul's Gospel lies in these central chapters of Romans; this is Paul's preaching of the good news, and that message can still shape our preaching today to all who suffer or are imprisoned by the forces of our world. It is easy to feel overwhelmed by drives in the world today—by the impersonality of huge bureaucracies, by the power of modern technology, by the reduction of people to statistics by government and modern institutions. But in God's eyes we are valued, chosen, and fought for. Who or what can possibly be against us that we should fear or despair?

CYCLE C

Genesis 15:5–12, 17–18 Abraham put his faith in the Lord.

Philippians 3:17–4:1 Christ will transfigure these wretched bodies of ours into copies of his glorious body.

Luke 9:28–36 As Jesus prayed, the aspect of his face was changed and his clothing became brilliant as lightning.

The first reading reminds us we are a people of the promise. God has reached out to Abraham and through Christ to all people with that covenant of abundance. In Abraham's day, that wealth was expressed as descendents who would be numerous as the stars and a land to be given them. What shape does this same promise hold for us and for our community today? How do we experience God's abundance in our lives?

Do we trust in this promise, or do we live in constant fear that God will not take care of us? How do we help one another to deeper trust in the Lord's promise? And how do we share with those outside our community that gift of prosperity we have, so that they too might come to know this wondrous God?

The Transfiguration provides another image for our reflection. This gospel looks forward to the conclusion of Lent and the Easter mystery. At Easter the full glory of

Christ is revealed. That glory is also seen at other times, such as on the mountaintop. The glory of Christ is all we have to share with the world. It is the good news. We acknowledge that glory in the resurrection, but where do we find it in our lives today?

Many of us have also been to the mountaintop. Studies show that a significant number of Americans have had mystical experiences. But our culture does not encourage us to speak of them. Often even our church is skeptical about such experiences. Yet such direct experience of God and God's love is sought by an overwhelming number of people Christian and non-Christian alike.

Part of evangelization is to create a place for people to be able to share such experiences. The glory of God is as present today as at any time in the past. How can our community offer a safe place where people might reflect upon such experiences and deepen their understanding of what God is doing in their lives and in our community? What are some experiences of the mountaintop for you and for our parish this past year?

Luke says that Jesus learns from the Transfiguration that he must go to Jerusalem to die. What do our experiences on the mountaintop reveal that we must do next to follow Jesus?

Third Sunday of Lent

CYCLE A

Exodus 17:3–7 Give us water to drink.

Romans 5:1–2, 5–8 The love of God has been poured into our hearts by the Holy Spirit which has been given to us.

John 4:5–42 The water that I shall give will turn into a spring of eternal life.

Jesus' meeting with the Samaritan woman provides a marvelous model for evangelization. First, he goes to her land. He does not wait for her to find him; he goes out to find her. We cannot wait for people to come to us. We must venture forth from our church to find them wherever they are.

Then, when she approaches the well Jesus begins to talk to her. He does not wait for her to initiate a conversation. Notice that he speaks to her about what she is doing. She is going to the well and he asks her for water. He begins a discussion of water that leads to the living water. The woman wants such water, and she begins to turn toward Jesus hoping he might be able to supply it.

When we engage our culture we must address it about its own concerns. We engage it in dialogue around common issues. And in that dialogue we will be able to indicate some Christian values in such a way that they might attract the person or group to want to know more. Like Jesus, we are making friends and inviting people rather than arguing with them.

As the dialogue goes on, Jesus demonstrates that he knows all about the woman and that he accepts her; he doesn't reject her as her fellow townspeople have. He speaks to her of her own heritage and traditions in such a way that he shows her the way to himself. But again he leads her in such a way that she perceives an invitation to pursue her quest rather than simply feeling she is wrong and therefore at fault. The underlying tone Jesus uses throughout this dialogue is one of engagement with the person on her own level, an invitation to explore a deeper level which will bring her closer to acknowledging the Christ.

CYCLE B

Exodus 20:1–17 The law was given through Moses.

1 Corinthians 1:22–25 We are preaching a crucified Christ, a scandal to people, but to those who have been called, the wisdom of God.

John 2:13–25 Destroy this sanctuary and in three days I will raise it up.

To be effective evangelizers, we need to understand and appreciate the power of images. In a real sense images save and heal us. The gospel today shows us how easy it is to misunderstand symbols. The people assume that Jesus is speaking of the temple of bricks and stones, whereas he really is speaking of the temple that is his body.

Our faith is filled with such images, which can refer to many things: the temple as our body, the temple as church. The images shift and change as they pass on to us the saving Word. There is no easy formula we can use to preach the gospel. We have experienced how Jesus has raised up our bodies into new life. We must then, in whatever way we can, share our experience of being raised up. The most direct approach may not be the most effective. Some of the most effective evangelization has been done through stories or films that do not mention Jesus at all but speak the Word nonetheless. Think of Charles Dickens's *A Christmas Carol.* He does not speak of Jesus, but his story of Scrooge communicates the Christian theme of love for the poor.

CYCLE C

Exodus 3:1–8, 13–15 This is what you must say to the children of Israel: "I am has sent me to you."

1 Corinthians 10:1–6, 10–12 All this that happened to the people of Moses in the desert was written for our benefit.

Luke 13:1–9 Unless you repent you will all perish as they did.

The second reading and the gospel speak of repentance, which is a major Lenten theme. First Jesus answers questions concerning people who have died. Were they any worse than others? No. But we are all in need of repentance, and unless we repent we all shall die. God's call is to life, but we are headed for death. Lent gives us a chance to look at our lives and turn our minds toward Christ.

Jesus tells the parable of the fig tree. The master has come three years in a row and found no fruit. He is about to cut it down when the vinedresser pleads for one more year. This is a marvelous image of God's mercy. God is always willing to give us another chance.

Many think of God as a stern judge, yet that is not the image Jesus gives us. Today, many people think of Christianity as a judgmental religion. Our evangelization task in the light of this misinformation is to promote the God of mercy. Our God wills no one to be lost. As a church, we reach out to everyone with God's mercy and invitation to turn away from death to life.

Fourth Sunday of Lent

CYCLE A

1 Samuel 16:1,6–7,10–13 In the presence of the Lord God, they anointed David king of Israel.

Ephesians 5:8–14 Rise from the dead, and Christ will shine on you.

John 9:1–41 The blind man went off and washed himself and came away with his sight restored.

The underlying theme of the gospel today is blindness. But there is considerable irony, because the man who was blind in the beginning sees quite well in the end. He sees that Jesus is the Christ. Those who could see in the beginning—the Pharisees—are shown to be blind by Jesus in the end. The metaphor of blindness serves as a key image in the gospel.

We see it again in a hymn such as "Amazing Grace," which says, "I was blind but now I see." This phrase could serve as a meditation on how to speak the good news. The gospel brings light into darkness. How has it done this for us? We all have stories of blindness being healed. Some of the elect today especially see the ways we were blind to the truth and how Jesus and his message have helped us see. Our society, largely through the gospel, has come to see the blindness of racism and prejudice, and has begun the slow journey toward equality and justice. What other ways is the light dispelling our blindness as individuals and as a faith community?

CYCLE B

2 Chronicles 36:14–17, 19–23 They ridiculed the prophets of God until at last his wrath rose so high, there was no remedy.

Ephesians 2:4–10 When we were dead through sins, God brought us to life.

John 3:14–21 God loved the world so much that God gave his only Son.

The second reading emphasizes God's mercy toward us and the gospel God's love of us. These must ground all our evangelization. We have been called to be Christians through absolutely no merit of our own but only because God loves us and has had mercy upon us. Everything we have is a gift flowing from this mercy and love.

Let us examine our lives for examples of God's mercy and love to us. How has God been merciful to us as a believing community? What crises have we survived because of God's mercy and love? Let this be a basis of our sharing the gospel. And of course the most obvious sign of this love and mercy is Jesus himself. John says Jesus was lifted up on the cross so that all might be able to see him and realize God's mercy toward us. How has the cross spoken to you personally of God's infinite mercy and love?

CYCLE C

Josiah 5:9, 10–12 The people of God went to the promised land and there kept the passover.

2 Corinthians 5:17–21 God reconciled us to himself through Christ.

Luke 15:1–3,11–32 Your brother here was dead and has come to life.

Saint Paul speaks of the ministry of reconciliation that was Christ's and that we have ourselves experienced and are now commissioned to provide to others. Evangelization is reconciliation. We are summoned to heal the wounds of division. How are we peacemakers in our community?

Luke tells the story of the prodigal son and continues the theme of reconciliation. It is easy for us to identify with the younger son. We can see times when we have sinned, and it is comforting to know that there is forgiveness available. But what of the elder son? How do we feel about forgiveness when we have been responsible while we see others as irresponsible? There is a lot of anger and meanness in our country today. We all have groups of people whom we feel are getting away with things whether it be welfare mothers or international corporations. Yet our ministry is not one of blame but of reconciliation and justice.

The story of the two brothers also speaks to a major aspect of our reconciliation ministry: our brothers and sisters who are alienated from the church. We all know people who used to be Catholics. Are we comfortable sharing our faith with them? Do they know that we are practicing Catholics? Are we willing to answer their questions?

We do not want to drag them home. That is not what happens in the parable, but the younger son does realize that he would be better off at home than where he is. Are we getting that message across to the alienated Catholics whom we know? Do we share how we manage to be Catholic and modern people at the same time? How do we as a parish promote this message?

Fifth Sunday of Lent

CYCLE A

Ezekiel 37:12–14 I shall put my spirit in you, and you will live.

Romans 8:8–11 If the Spirit of him who raised Jesus from the dead is living in you then he will give life to your own mortal bodies.

John 11:1–45 I am the resurrection and the life.

The story of the raising of Lazarus provides the basic image of the good news. Jesus raises death into life. The gospel proclaims that out of every death, God wills a resurrection. We all have experienced such resurrections in our own life and in our community. Those of us who are over fifty years old have seen an old church die and a new church being born. Who would have thought that the Catholic Church could change so greatly in only thirty years after centuries of doing things the same way?

But didn't the changes bring with them all sorts of problems? Certainly Catholics have many problems today. Consider Lazarus. How was it for him to be raised from the dead? What was it like to return to life? What profound changes and pains he must have endured!

Our gospel does not promise to make everything easy. It promises new life, and life always brings problems and mysteries with it. Jesus does not solve the mysteries of living; he shows us a way through those mysteries that does not do away with them but rather reveals their wonder and glory. When we proclaim the good news, we do not need to have all the answers; we do not have to have our house or our church in order. All we need do is witness, like Lazarus, to the power that has raised us from the dead and continues to do so.

CYCLE B

Jeremiah 31:31–34 The days are coming when I will make a new covenant with Israel and I will forgive their iniquity.

Hebrews 5:7–9 He learned to obey and become for all the source of eternal salvation.

John 12:20–33 If a grain of wheat falls on the ground and dies, it yields a rich harvest.

We can sense God's love in today's reading from Jeremiah. The law will be written on our hearts. We shall be God's people and we shall know God intimately. The gospel deepens our understanding of that love as we realize how Jesus is willing to allow himself to be put to death for us. He is willing to die so that we might grow. This love of God is the crux of the good news. In whatever way possible, we need to tell stories of experiencing this love in our own lives and in that of our community.

Such love draws us towards God. Everyone loves a love story. Our gospel is the greatest of all love stories. Many love stories have tragic endings—the lovers die. Yet they make us feel good somehow. On some level, the death is not really tragic: the lovers triumph over death or whatever threatens to separate them. The gospel story—in one sense tragic, in another not—reveals why we feel this way. Jesus dies, and yet in dying gains the world.

CYCLE C

Isaiah 43:16–21 I am doing a new thing and I will give drink to my people.

Philippians 3:8–14 Because of Christ, I look upon everything else as useless in order to gain him.

John 8:1–11 Let the one without sin be the first to throw a stone.

Human beings tend to live in the past. But to do so overwhelms us. Both the first reading and the gospel speak of forgetting and forgiveness. "God is doing something new!" exclaims Isaiah. Christians have something new to bring to the world, something for which the world longs.

The world does not need to be reminded of its past, or its sins. Rather it needs to hear the new things that God brings into our midst. Of course it is easier to blame than to forgive and forget. Yet forgiveness when it truly happens is an astonishing event.

Think of the times when you have been forgiven. Let us bring this new thing of forgiveness to our community. Are we able in this Lenten season to look at our lives and forgive those who have hurt us? Do we extend an open invitation to people to come hear the good news? And how do we assure people that they will not be judged or condemned but forgiven and healed by this new thing the Lord is doing?

Paul speaks of redemption as an ongoing process. Redemption, forgiveness, and God's new action occur in the cross and resurrection of Jesus. Here is where and how forgiveness happens. Jesus leaves absolutely nothing hanging over us. Our past is totally buried in his grave. Yet although we are in truth redeemed already, yet we struggle to finish the course and grasp the prize. We are not perfect yet and shall not be till that final day. Let us examine ourselves and our community in the shadow of the cross. How can we be more a sign of forgiveness and a promise of a new day for our world?

Passion Sunday—Cycles A, B, and C

Procession:

A: Matthew 21:1–11 Blessed is he who comes in the name of the Lord.

B: Mark 11:1–10 Blessed is the one who comes in the name of the Lord.

C: Luke 19:28–40 Blessed is he who comes in the name of the Lord.

Isaiah 50:4–7 I did not cover my face against insult and I know I will not be ashamed.

Philippians 2:6–11 He humbled himself to become like us and God raised him on high.

Passion:

A: Matthew 26:14–27:66

B: Mark 14:1–15:47

C: Luke 22:14–23:56

The events we celebrate this week are the very center of the good news we are given to share with the world. Today we remember Jesus' Passion. We recall how he went from acclamation by the crowds on Palm Sunday to betrayal and death on Good Friday. The gospel story touches on the extremes of human existence. God took on human life in all its moments from birth, yes, even to death. In doing so God shows us the way to be human—not by escaping or trying to deny our situation, but by embracing it.

Year after year we return to the events of this week to be renewed. How does this story touch our life this year? What does it say to our illness, to the discord in our family life, to the present life of the church? What death is God dying this year in our life, in our community, and in our church? How does God raise us up from that death? How is the story of Christ's Passion, death, and resurrection being retold in the details of our life today? If we can see how it is unfolding in our life and community, we can receive the gospel that God is giving us to proclaim to our time and our culture. We retreat into Holy Week to discover the mysterious way in which God is touching our lives today, so that like the disciples at Easter we too may go forth renewed to proclaim good news.

4

Season of Easter

Easter Sunday— Cycles A, B, and C

Acts of the Apostles 10:34, 37–43 We have eaten and drunk with him after his resurrection from the dead.

Colossians 3:1–4 Look for the things that are in heaven, where Christ is.

John 20:1–9 The teaching of scripture is that he must rise from the dead.

Our gospel speaks of Mary Magdalene going to the tomb and finding the stone moved away. She has seen a sign of the resurrection. No one witnesses the actual resurrection. We are all asleep when it happens. But we all perceive signs of it in the scriptures, the church, our world, our lives.

When Mary sees the stone rolled away, she immediately goes to seek out Peter to share the news. Then Peter and the beloved disciple come to view for themselves. They go into the tomb and see the winding sheets, which are simply another sign. At this point the beloved disciple believes. And they go forth to tell others.

This is how the resurrection blossoms. No one sees it firsthand. Yet we all behold the evidence: in the arrival of spring, in the testimony of scripture, in the stories of the new Christians who were born this night, in the healing we have experienced in our lives.

But if we leave the resurrection there in the event it is incomplete. Every resurrection narrative includes a going forth to tell the good news. So it was then; so it is now. We must tell the story of the victory of life over death. We can tell it as our story, as the story of others in our community, as the story of our church, which does everything possible to kill itself yet keeps being resurrected. But tell it we must, or we are left as we might be at the end of this gospel with an empty tomb, burial wrappings on the ground, and a failure to understand the scripture that Christ must rise from the dead. Can we really say we understand this scripture if we fail to proclaim it from the rooftops?

Second Sunday of Easter

CYCLE A

Acts of the Apostles 2:42–47 The faithful lived together and owned everything in common.

1 Peter 1:3–9 He has given us a new birth as his children, by raising Jesus Christ from the dead.

John 20:19–31 After eight days Jesus came in and stood among them.

The example of these early Christians in the first reading is very powerful. These people trusted the gospel to such an extent that they left their individual lives behind, pooled their resources, shared all things in common, and withdrew on the basis of need. They ate their meals in common and shared daily in the breaking of the bread and prayers.

While today, for the most part only religious orders follow the lifestyle of these first Christians, we as a church are still defined by our prayer and by the Eucharist. The Eucharist is possibly the most powerful attraction toward the church. Again and again catechumens and candidates testify that they were attracted to us first through the atmosphere of prayer they found in our churches and through our celebration of the Eucharist.

Let us ask ourselves about our prayer life. We do not pray to attract people to the gospel, but that is certainly a factor in people's conversions. Are you a person of prayer? Is it something you hide, or simply a part of your life? It is definitely not something to flaunt; that would be a perversion. But do our friends and neighbors experience us as a person, a family, a people of prayer?

Peter tells us that we suffer so that our faith may by its genuineness lead to praise, glory, and honor when Jesus Christ appears. How can we live our lives in this way? How can we witness in the midst of suffering that we live in hope of consolation and comfort? There are many reasons today to be pessimistic.

But the Christian trusts that all is in God's care. In our own lives and in our society we can be a source of hope rather than despair. A sign of this hope is the joy we express. Peter conveyed it through his praise; how do we as individuals and as a community embody the joy of the resurrection in the midst of our troubles?

Finally, the gospel tells of the mission of forgiveness entrusted to the apostles. That same mission has been passed down to us. We are a focus of forgiveness in this world. We readily forgive one another. We are open to those who are alienated, and we offer them God's reconciliation. We are called to be signs of forgiveness in our world; we are not here to judge, but to extend to all the wonderful forgiveness of God upon which the good news is founded.

CYCLE B

Acts of the Apostles 4:32–35 The whole group was united heart and soul.

1 John 5:1–6 Anyone begotten by God has already overcome the world.

John 20:19–31 After eight days Jesus came in and stood among them.

In today's first reading, the community itself is an evangelizing sign to the world. They pool their goods in common; they live as one heart and mind. How is our community a sign of God's love? Is our community welcoming? Is it filled with love? Does it manifest God's generosity? Actions proclaim the good news much more powerfully than do words.

We are begotten by God, as John says. How do we show this royal birth to others? The greatest gift we share in common is the Holy Spirit. This Spirit has been poured out upon our community. With the Spirit we participate in God's great work of reconciliation. Our community is a sign of that reconciliation. We experienced it when the church reached out to include us. How do we show forth that Spirit of reconciliation to others?

Perhaps, like Thomas, we hesitate because we have not seen with our own eyes. We think how privileged Thomas was because he got to touch the wounds of Jesus. But have we not seen many signs of Jesus' resurrection? Two thousand years of history are strewn with the signs of his victory over sin and death. We have the example and testimony of the saints that Jesus is triumphant.

The gospel ends by telling of the many other signs Jesus has performed in the presence of his disciples. What are those signs? Who are those disciples? Are they just the original twelve, or do they include the millions who have followed throughout history? The signs continue into our day—they appear in our own lives and in the life of our community. We too, like Thomas, have seen the Lord. Now let us, like Thomas, share our good news with others who have not yet met the Lord.

CYCLE C

Acts of the Apostles 5:12–16 The numbers of men and women who came to believe in the Lord increased steadily.

Revelation 1:9–11, 12–13, 17–19 I was dead and now I am to live for ever and ever.

John 20:19–31 After eight days Jesus came in and stood among them.

Fear is mentioned or implied in all three readings today. In the first reading, people held back from joining these Christians even though they held them in high esteem. Jesus tells John in the second reading, "There is nothing to fear." In the gospel, the disciples are hiding for fear and are assured by the appearance of Jesus.

There is a tremendous amount of fear in contemporary society. Fear leads to paralysis and disaster. When we are afraid we do rash things; we are easily manipulated. Easter tells us that we need not fear death. And if we need not fear death, what could possibly make us afraid?

One way of carrying the Easter message is in the assuaging of fear. Do we try to alleviate fear when we find it or do we add to it? What part does fear play in our own life and vision of the world? Is our church a fearful or a hopeful and confident community? How can we help one another and our neighbors to cast out fear in the light of Easter?

Third Sunday of Easter

CYCLE A

Acts of the Apostles 2:14, 22–33 It was impossible for him to be held by the power of Hades.

1 Peter 1:17–21 The ransom that was paid to free you was the blood of the Lamb, Jesus Christ.

Luke 24:13–35 They had recognized him at the breaking of the bread.

In a sense, our whole culture is similar to the two disciples walking on the way to Emmaeus. There is practically no one in America today who does not know the gospel story: that Jesus died and was resurrected on the third day. These two disciples also know that story. What they do not know is how it applies to Jesus and to them. And what our culture, and sometimes we ourselves, do not know today is exactly what relevance the resurrection of Jesus has for us.

In Jesus' cross all sins are reconciled and the fear of death is taken away. We celebrate that redemption each Sunday in the Eucharist. If we celebrate it in a knowing way, people will sense the presence of Jesus among us just as the disciples did at Emmaeus. But if our liturgy is but an empty shell, a bored rehearsal of a too well-known story, how do we or others sense the presence of Jesus there? We keep it from becoming empty when we, like the disciples, tell one another just how Jesus is living and moving in our lives. We must share this good news first with one another before we can share it with the world. The disciples jumped up and ran back to the others to speak the good news. In what ways can we tell one another about the presence and activity of the risen Christ in our lives and community?

CYCLE B

Acts of the Apostles 3:13–15, 17–19 You have killed the prince of life; God, however, raised him from the dead.

1 John 2:1–5 Jesus Christ is the sacrifice that takes away our sins, and those of the whole world.

Luke 24:35–48 It was written that the Christ would suffer and on the third day rise from the dead.

How do we become an evangelizing people? By keeping God's commandments. What are these commandments? They are the way of life we witness in Jesus. The commandments enjoin us to be loving, forgiving, compassionate to the poor and outcast. In observing the commandments, we model ourselves on Jesus and become more like him. Once our community shines forth with Jesus' face, the work of evangelization will flow from us.

But to reflect Jesus takes work. We need to study the scriptures together as did the disciples so that Jesus may open our minds. As we grow in our comprehension of scripture, we open ourselves more to God's transforming power. As we burn more and more with the light of Christ, we show all people the God who has saved us and whom we have come to know. And we enable others to encounter our God as well.

It was very hard for the disciples to believe that Jesus had risen from the dead. They were incredulous. For most of us, belief in Jesus' resurrection is not the main stumbling block. We have difficulty believing that the resurrection takes place within us and within our community.

We are the Easter people. We are not talking about some episode that happened two thousand years ago, but an event happening at this moment within us. To overcome our incredulity, we must undergo the same education as the disciples. We need to spend time with Jesus, read the scriptures with him, pray with him, and see the signs of his presence among us. He will strengthen our faith. Once we are confident he is alive in us we will be able, like the disciples, to announce and demonstrate this good news to our neighbors.

CYCLE C

Acts of the Apostles 5:27–32,40–41 We are witnesses to all this, we and the Holy Spirit whom God has given to those who obey.

Revelation 5:11–14 The Lamb that was sacrificed is worthy to be given power, wealth, glory, and blessing.

John 21:1–19 Jesus stepped forward, took the bread and gave it to them, and did the same with the fish.

We see in the first two readings how Christians by nature testify and glorify. In the first reading, the disciples are filled with joy that they had been ill treated by the Sanhedrin. The gospel is good news, but it is not necessarily what we or others want to hear. We are sent to bring good news to the poor in a society that increasingly scapegoats them. Are we willing to speak the truth like the disciples, or do we not wish to rock the boat? It is easy to speak against those who have no power.

But we Christians today are powerful; will we use our power to speak for the powerless? And will we rejoice when we are ill treated? Revelation describes the heavenly liturgy where songs of praise rise to God. Our liturgy is the most powerful tool of evangelization we have been given. Is it filled with joyful praise? It is a ministry of evangelization simply to sing out in church so that God is praised and others may come to know God's glory.

Fourth Sunday of Easter

CYCLE A

Acts of the Apostles 2:14, 36–41 God has made Jesus both Lord and Christ.

1 Peter 2:20–25 You had gone astray but now you have come back to the shepherd and guardian of your souls.

John 10:1–10 I am the gate of the sheepfold.

When Jesus uses the figure of the sheepfold in today's gospel, John says that the disciples did not understand what he was saying. And the situation may be even more true for us. The Good Shepherd has become a key symbol of Jesus. But we live in a culture where few of us have ever seen a shepherd, let alone become familiar with one. For us the word evokes romantic Christian images. For Jesus' audience, the reality of shepherds was hardly that of Christmas cards. It was as down to earth as you could get. As we speak the good news to our own times, we need to find new images with which to capture the excitement and reality of the gospel.

Here he is telling us that when we hear the real shepherd something within us knows that this is the one to trust and to follow. Something within us resonates to the call of the real shepherd. In preaching the gospel today, amid all the other competing gospels, how can we help people discern that, yes, this is the truth. This is in accord with who I really am and how things actually are.

There are competing gospels—gospels that claim to be Christian and those that do not. Which is the true good news? When have you heard good news that rings true to you in the depths of your being? What is the good news that our culture needs to hear that will awaken our neighbors to the truth of God's love and care for all? And what image might capture that truth?

CYCLE B

Acts of the Apostles 4:8–12 This is the only name by which we can be saved.

1 John 3:1–2 We shall see God as God is.

John 10:11–18 The good shepherd lays down his life for his sheep.

The world did not recognize the first Christians because, as John says, it did not recognize the Son. But why does the world not recognize us? We are not some tiny community like the first churches. We are quite visible to the world. We are one of the largest world religions.

Why doesn't the world identify us as the community of Jesus? If the world sees the church as one of the most powerful institutions, how can it recognize that church as the community of Jesus? We must be about the work of Jesus: a work of compassion rather than power.

The gospel speaks of the good shepherd—an image Jesus often employed to speak of himself. The shepherd was not powerful in the society of Jesus' day. He was on the margins of the community. He spent most of his time alone with his sheep. He was often suspect; he might be a thief or a trespasser. Yet Jesus sees himself as a shepherd: one of the overlooked. A person who spends his life in service to his sheep. And Jesus takes the image even further when he announces he will give his life for his sheep.

As Jesus' community, how are we good shepherds? For whom do we care? For whom do we sacrifice? How do we reach out to the forgotten people of today and make flesh the love of God? We are charged by Jesus to manifest his concern for people. If we are seen as a community of concern and care, people will recognize us not simply as the Christian church, but as the people among whom Jesus still lives and ministers.

CYCLE C

Acts of the Apostles 13:14, 43–52 Many became believers.

Revelation 7:9, 14–17 The Lamb who is on the throne will be their shepherd and will lead them to springs of living water.

John 10:27–30 I give my sheep eternal life.

The first reading tells of Paul's and Barnabas's efforts to bring the good news to Israel. But Israel is not willing to hear a new message. The good news is never something that we can say we have heard and to which we have responded. God's word, the gospel, is always a present word. Each time we really hear the gospel, we hear something new, something we have not heard before. The good news stretches us. If it makes us complacent, if it gives us the satisfaction that we are the in crowd and those other poor people just do not have a clue, we are in danger of being in the same situation as the Jews in this reading.

When we evangelize, we do not have a prepackaged product to sell to as many people as possible. Rather we offer an invitation to enter into the presence of the living Christ. In his presence we are all transformed and will continue to be transformed as long as we live. It is a temptation for Christians to feel they already have experienced the gospel and committed to it, and so resist the pull of God to move forward toward the kingdom. Yet if we do not follow God's call in our lives and situations today, we are in danger of being left behind.

Fifth Sunday of Easter

CYCLE A

Acts of the Apostles 6:1–7 They elected seven filled with the Spirit and wisdom.

1 Peter 2:4–9 You are a chosen race, a royal priesthood.

John 14:1–12 I am the way, the truth and the life.

The reading from Acts shows how the early community responded creatively to crises as they arose. When the numbers made it impossible for the apostles to do the table ministry, others were chosen for that service. We are a community first. We are all bound together, and we depend upon one another. So it must be with our efforts at evangelization. We must look at our community—who has what gifts—and then find ways that each member can use his or her gifts in the service of the entire community. Some people will be able to articulate the faith to inquirers; others are gifted at making people feel welcome and connecting them with others; others find their calling in work and might organize and perform service projects for the larger community as a sign of Christ in society.

Evangelization has many different facets and dimensions. It is not just a matter of knocking on doors, or preaching on street corners. Let us come together and discern the ways in which Christ might be made present in our society and then distinguish which of our members' talents will help us accomplish these tasks.

CYCLE B

Acts of the Apostles 9:26–31 He explained how the Lord appeared to Saul and spoke to him on his journey.

1 John 3:18–24 His commandments are these: that we believe and that we love one another.

John 15:1–8 Whoever who lives in me, and I in them, bears much fruit.

John tells us that we must live the gospel; it is not enough simply to talk about it. We prove our commitment when we put it into practice. Actions are much more powerful than words alone. In the first reading we see a changed Saul. Now he is converted to Jesus. But the other Christians remember all too vividly his past actions against the church. They do not trust him. It will take time for Paul to win their trust through new deeds.

To do the works of Jesus shows that Jesus and his spirit are alive in us. Both the second reading and the gospel speak of this intimate connection with Jesus. The gospel uses the image of the vine and the branches. When we proclaim the good news to others, we are simply doing what Jesus himself did. And when we proclaim the good news, we give Jesus the chance to act within us. We cannot be Christians without allowing Jesus to act within us. As the gospel says, whoever lives in me...will produce abundantly. Such abundance is one of the signs of being in Christ.

CYCLE C

Acts of the Apostles 14:21–27 They assembled the church and gave an account of all that God had done with them.

Revelation 21:1–5 God will wipe away all the tears from their eyes.

John 13:31–33, 34–35 I give you a new commandment: love one another.

The second reading and the gospel present two key themes of the good news we have to offer one another and our neighbors. At the end of the Book of Revelation

Jesus says, "Behold, I make all things new." This is a powerful message for our day when things seem to be disintegrating and falling apart. We live in times of confusion, of rampant violence and crime, of deteriorating values. In many ways our situation is not much different from the Roman Empire in John's time. The difference is that then the Christian community was only a small group of people. But in spite of the evident decay and rot, Christ brings a message of hope. In Christ all is made new. Rather than decrying our failing society, how might we Christians help to make things new and bring this message of hope to people today?

The gospel provides the second great theme of evangelization. Beyond all the words we utter or the arguments we might use to convince people of the truth of the gospel, the way we live our lives is by far the best means. If people see us as an accepting, inviting, and loving community they will be drawn toward us. Indeed the experience of warmth in a Christian community overcomes a multitude of objections or doubts people may have about various aspects of the church. They experience the love of Jesus alive in us and know they have come home.

Sixth Sunday of Easter

CYCLE A

Acts of the Apostles 8:5–8, 14–17 They laid hands on them, and they received the Holy Spirit.

1 Peter 3:15–18 In the body he was put to death, in the spirit he was raised to life.

John 14:15–21 I shall ask the Father and God will give you another Advocate.

Peter today gives us a wonderful description of the evangelist—and we are each of us evangelists. Begin by keeping Christ in your heart and honoring Christ there. Evangelization is founded upon our own and our community's continuing conversion. If that constant conversion ceases, our message will dry up and be worthless. We cannot do anything if we do not hold Christ first in our hearts.

Then we must always be ready to show inquirers what our hope depends on. Why do we live in hope when we could just as easily and more reasonably live in despair considering what is happening in the world? What is the reason for our hope? What is the reason for your hope? How does Jesus give you hope? Are you willing to explain if you are asked?

Peter goes on to say how we are to share. We share first of all with gentleness. We have all encountered people who almost force themselves or what they want to sell upon us. This is not how we are to share the gospel. When a person asks us to partake, let us be gentle. Let us share only as much as the person asks for. Let us be aware of how they receive our message. Let us be concerned for them first. How are they hearing what we say? Are they hearing us correctly?

And we share with reverence. Our reverence is first for Christ for he is our Lord—the source of our joy. But our reverence is also and just as much for the person who is asking. For they too are Christ—the Holy Spirit breathes in them also. We are simply helping them to see this Spirit that gives them life and to name Jesus as we have.

CYCLE B

Acts of the Apostles 10:25–26, 34–35, 44–48 The Holy Spirit came down on all the listeners.

1 John 4:7–10 God is love.

John 15:9–17 A man can have no greater love than to lay down his life for his friends.

The first lesson today demonstrates what happens when we evangelize. First, Cornelius shows great reverence for Peter. The message we bear is one of great awe and majesty. We bear good news, and when people first hear the gospel they are overwhelmed. They may mistake us for our message. But as Peter reassures Cornelius, I am only human myself. Do not confuse me for the word I bring.

Let us not forget what a great message we bear. We may have lived with the gospel for many years. We may have grown comfortable with it. But it is overwhelming news, and when others first hear it, we have the opportunity to hear it again with them as though for the first time.

The second lesson is that God shows no partiality. As we engage in evangelization, we will be constantly surprised by this unbiased God. People hear us and receive the gospel regardless of their pasts or of who they are. The other side of this is the mystery of how some people simply cannot hear the good news no matter what kind of preparation we may think they have had. People raised in Catholic homes may prove quite deaf to the gospel. This is not their or our fault; it is part of the mystery of whom Jesus calls to be his follower.

And finally we must recognize with Peter that when we see the grace of God working within a person or a community, we ought not to put obstacles in the way. The early Jewish Christians felt that the Gentiles should be circumcised before they could be baptized. But Peter saw the Spirit working in these people and realized that they should not be denied baptism. Similarly we might have ideas about what a person should be in order to be called to Jesus. Give up all such ideas. When you see the Holy Spirit drawing that person to Jesus, acknowledge it and help the person toward the faith.

CYCLE C

Acts of the Apostles 15:1–2, 22–29 It seemed right to the Holy Spirit and to us not to burden you beyond what is essential.

Revelation 21:10–14, 22–23 He showed me the holy city coming down out of heaven.

John 14:23–29 The Holy Spirit will teach you everything and remind you of all I have said to you.

In the first reading from Acts, we meet a situation where people are concerned that new Christians meet all the requirements. After all, the faith should not be watered down. This behavior is quite human, and we see it in many areas of faith life. Some parents are still concerned that their children are not really learning the faith because children today are not forced to memorize all the things that their parents had to memorize. How can we be sure they are really getting it? Some catechumenate directors focus upon the doctrines and rules of the faith to make sure that these new Catholics are properly educated.

But rules, doctrines, and formulas are not faith. Faith is a direct trust and reliance upon God. Faith invites us into a relationship with God. Uncertainty and ambiguity are part of the faith experience, not opposed to it. A catechumenate or religious education community properly invites people to enter into and experience our continuing pilgrimage with our God.

Similarly, our task of evangelization is not to present the various beliefs, doctrines, or morals of Christianity, but to invite people to meet the living God. As Paul realizes, the Holy Spirit does not want to lay unnecessary burdens upon people, but rather to liberate them from whatever enslaves. So too as we invite people to share our faith, let us keep the essential core in sight—the encounter with the living God. All these other things are helpful, useful, meaningful, but not necessarily necessary.

Ascension of the Lord—
Cycles A, B, and C

Acts of the Apostles 1:1–11 Why are you standing here looking into the sky? Jesus has been taken into heaven.

Ephesians 1:17–23 God made Jesus to sit at his right hand in heaven.

Matthew 28:16–20 All authority in heaven and on earth has been given to me.

The feast of the Ascension is an important one for evangelizers. As bearers of the good news, we continually feel we are not adequate to such an important task. But the action of today's feast assures us that God knows what God is doing. Not only does God love us, knowing us through and through, with all our strengths as well as our weaknesses. But God, knowing all of this, chooses us to be the messengers of his good news to others.

If Jesus had stayed on earth, he could very well have continued his ministry of announcing the good news himself. But he goes to join the Father precisely because he wishes us to continue his ministry. Sometimes we may not know what we are doing in our ministry. But let us rest assured that God knows what God is doing; and God is perfectly happy to allow the ministry of evangelization to fall to us.

Seventh Sunday of Easter

CYCLE A

Acts of the Apostles 1:12–14 All of them were joined together in the upper room, continuously praying.

1 Peter 4:13–16 It is a blessing for you when they insult you for bearing the name of Christ.

John 17:1–11 Jesus raised his eyes to heaven and said: Father, glorify your Son.

As Peter reminds us, suffering is part of the experience of being a Christian, and suffering forms a part of our evangelization. We often show forth Christ best in our weakness rather than in our strength. When we are strong our words may be fine and noble, but there may be no real experience behind them. Yet when we are suffering, when we are down, when we are weak, often then the Spirit shines most through us. The sufferings of people in developing counties and their faith despite such pain can speak louder than our words from a place of comfort. And the faith of a person dying is often more able to communicate the presence of Christ than our faith when we are in control. All members of the Christian community are evangelists—the articulate, the tongue-tied, the very old and the very young, the sick and the healthy. Sometimes a child's innocence and joy can cut through an adult's cynicism in a way that the most persuasive argument cannot.

CYCLE B

Acts of the Apostles 1:15–17, 20–26 We must therefore choose someone who has been with us the whole time, and he can act with us as a witness to his resurrection.

1 John 4:11–16 Whoever lives in love, lives in God and God in them.

John 17:11–19 Father, may they be one in us!

In Acts, the disciples gather to select Judas's successor to act as an apostle. Notice the qualification: He must be a witness to the resurrection. The same qualification applies to us. How have we experienced the resurrection flooding our life with light? We do not need to be present at the original resurrection. Paul certainly was not.

But we must have seen the risen Lord in our life. This is not hard to do. We can see him first of all in one another and especially among the neophytes who were baptized at Easter. Of course we witnessed the same event at our own baptisms, but most of us were too young to appreciate its fullness at that time. If you want a rich experience of resurrection, why not sponsor a catechumen and walk with him or her on the journey toward faith?

The most powerful witness to our faith as Christians is our love for one another, as John reminds us. God is love, and whoever abides in God abides in love. How does our community show its love for one another? How do we express our love for our neighborhood? How can people experience God's love through our church's presence in the community? Is this a place where people are fed, clothed, housed, made to feel welcome and important? These actions are some of the most powerful witnesses to our God.

CYCLE C

Acts of the Apostles 7:55–60 I can see the heavens thrown open and the Son of Man standing at the right hand of God.

Revelation 22:12–14, 16–17, 20 Come, Lord Jesus!

John 17:20–26 Father, may they be one in us!

A case could be made for Saint Stephen as the ultimate model for all evangelizers. Yes, he proclaims the good news. And he is rejected by the people, but he goes further. He actually lives the good news. The model for his life is Jesus himself. As Saint Luke tells the story, he is very much aware of Jesus' own death as the ground over which he weaves Stephen's martyrdom. Like Jesus, Stephen in his last words prays for those who persecute him. Which is the more powerful proclaiming of the gospel: telling the story, or living the story? So in our evangelization let us not rely overly on words and reason. How we live, how we treat one another, how we react toward those who spurn us evangelizes more than words can tell.

The gospel brings up another dimension of evangelization—the reconciliation of Christian communities. First, we must be clear that we are evangelizing for the gospel, not just for a particular church. Yes, we are Catholics and we believe that our community is the essence of what a Christian community is. But we proclaim Christ first and we proclaim him within a Catholic context. Thus our way of proclaiming is definitely colored by our Catholicism, but we proclaim Christ.

Part of our mission of evangelization is also to reduce the scandal of Christian disunity. How might we cooperate with other Christians in proclaiming the gospel? In doing so we may learn to overcome our differences and find more clearly the presence of Christ.

Pentecost—Cycles A, B, and C

Acts of the Apostles 2:1–11 They were all filled with the Holy Spirit, and began to speak in different languages.

1 Corinthians 12:3–7, 12–13 In one Spirit we were all baptized, making one body.

John 20:19–23 As the Father sent me, so I send you. Receive the Holy Spirit.

The first two readings today both speak of variety and diversity. Acts tells of the disciples speaking the many languages of the Earth—addressing each group with the good news of Jesus in their native tongue.

As Catholics we have moved from a time when we worshiped only in the Latin language, which we said bound us together. The problem was that few of us, even among priests, really understood Latin. Today we celebrate in our own languages, but as American Catholics this creates other problems if we are sensitive. Although English is the common language of our country, many people are newly arrived and still feel most comfortable in their own languages.

Ideally, every Catholic service should have some of the feeling of the first Pentecost, where each hears good news in his or her native tongue. What a sign of welcome if some of our songs are in Spanish or Vietnamese or other languages of people in our community! Whether all of us know these languages is not the point; it is that we celebrate

Christ in whatever language people speak. Inclusiveness is a great sign of the kingdom and a wonderful invitation to come and feel at home with us.

The second reading speaks of the variety of gifts that manifest in our community. We are never alone or solitary as Christians; we are part of the body of Christ. If I cannot do something well, someone else has that talent. So as we proclaim our good news to the world let us show how all gifts are valued and welcomed in our community. James Joyce said of the Catholic Church, "Here comes everybody." That is exactly who Jesus calls us to be—inclusive and welcoming and rejoicing in all peoples, cultures, languages, and gifts.

Holy Trinity

CYCLE A

Exodus 34:4–6,7–9 The Lord God, ruler of all, merciful and loving.

2 Corinthians 13:11–13 The grace of our Lord Jesus Christ and the love of God and the fellowship of the Holy Spirit be with you all.

John 3:16–18 God sent his Son to save the world through him.

The dogma of the Holy Trinity lies at the heart of our faith. We believe that God is essentially love. But love always needs a beloved. So we understand God as a community of love: Father, Son, and Holy Spirit.

It is not a good idea to try to explain our belief in the Trinity to others when we begin to share the gospel with them. After all, this feast, coming after the feast of Pentecost, hints that the mystery of the Trinity is one of the last to unfold for us. But we can witness to Abba the unknowable origin of all that is, who yet draws so close to us that we call him "Daddy." And if we are asked who has given us permission to address God in this way we can point to Jesus and share his teachings concerning God. And when people ask us what sustains us in our faith, what enables us to believe and to live out Jesus' teachings, we can point to our heart and speak of God's Spirit dwelling there who gives us the courage and freedom to speak of God so intimately.

CYCLE B

Deuteronomy 4:32–34, 39–40 The Lord himself is God in heaven above and on earth below: there is no other.

Romans 8:14–17 You have received the Spirit that makes you God's own children, and in that Spirit we call God: Father, our Father!

Matthew 28:16–20 Baptize them in the name of the Father, and of the Son, and of the Holy Spirit.

The Trinity does nothing to deny or gloss over the reality of but one God. At times the doctrine confused people and some have seen the revelation to Muhammad as a corrective to the many doctrines and heresies floating about over the Near East concerning the Trinity. We worship but one God, as the first reading makes clear. And we should be careful in the way we speak about the Trinity and the way in which we pray, so that people are not confused by us. We approach God the Father in the Son and through the Holy Spirit. Jesus shows us the face of God, and the Spirit reveals in our hearts the experience of God, but all still turn to God the Father.

Our faith begins and lives, as John's Gospel makes clear, with the revelation of God's awesome love, which went so far as to give his Son to us. Here is the ultimate gift—Jesus—the proof of God's love. And that love is extended to us. And our greatest joy is to share that love with one another and with all people. The Trinity may be the unexplainable mystery at the heart of our faith, but the love that is revealed by this community of God leads us into its depths.

CYCLE C

Proverbs 8:22–31 Wisdom was born before the earth was made.

Romans 5:1–5 To God through Christ in the love which is poured out through the Spirit.

John 16:12–15 Whatever the Father has is mine. The Spirit will receive what I give and tell you about it.

We used to believe that the Trinity was the one doctrine that was unique to Christianity. Today, as we have come to know more of other faiths, we see that although they may not speak of God in exactly the same trinitarian language, the notion of trinity is prevalent in many traditions. Rather than being an obstacle to world unity, the Trinity may become a unifying concept.

Today's first reading speaks of wisdom, the firstborn of all creation. All religious traditions agree that they are searching for wisdom. We share this value already in common. More than that, all would agree that wisdom is precious, not easily come by, and to be celebrated wherever she appears. Evangelization means to proclaim the good news, but it does not necessarily imply that those who hear it will come to join our faith. They may be evangelized by us and so deepen their insight and appreciation of their own faith tradition. The ultimate goal of evangelization is to alert people to the love of God. How they move toward that love may be through the Christian church or it may be through their native traditions, but if they come to know God more deeply through our evangelization we will have been worthy servants of our Lord. Our task is not to convert, but to proclaim the good news that has enriched and deepened our life.

The Body and Blood of Christ

CYCLE A

Deuteronomy 8:2–3, 14–16 God gave you food which you and your ancestors did not know.

1 Corinthians 10:16–17 Though we are many, we form a single body because we share this one loaf.

John 6:51–58 My flesh is real food and my blood is real drink.

The Eucharist is the very center of our faith life. And our symbol-starved culture craves what we have. Many people have testified that they were drawn to the Catholic Church because of the Eucharist. This simple rite of bread and wine enshrines a sacred mystery that speaks powerfully not only to Christians but to everyone. After all, it takes one of the most basic and universal human actions—a common meal—and finds in it the presence of a loving God who gives himself to us as food and drink.

We hear of the good old days when the mystery of the Mass was so palpable. But even celebrated in our own language, with simplicity and reverence, that same unspeakable mystery shines forth. We gather together weekly, some of us daily, at this common table. Yes, it is a meal, but it is more than that. It speaks to us of the mystery at the heart of all human meals: of community, of love, of sacrifice (for the food we eat was once alive), and of love. Let us be eager to invite many guests to our table. Let everyone come to this table, which proclaims Christ's love for us to the point of sacrificing himself for our sake.

CYCLE B

Exodus 24:3–8 This is the blood of the covenant that the Lord has made with you.

Hebrews 9:11–15 The blood of Christ will purify our inner selves.

Mark 14:12–16, 22–26 This is my body. This is my blood.

Ask a convert to the Catholic faith what was the primary attraction and chances are the answer will be, "The Eucharist." The ordinary and extraordinary action of giving thanks and sharing bread and wine in the name of Jesus is our greatest treasure. The Church acknowledges this in the Liturgy Constitution of the Second Vatican Council. Ask yourself, Why do I remain a Roman Catholic? What draws you back to the church in times of crisis and times of celebration? Is it not the Eucharist? Catholics value this simple action so much that unlike our Orthodox brothers and sisters we celebrate it every day and sometimes more than once a day in any one parish.

If we were to try to describe briefly who Jesus is, what better way to communicate the person and the message than in Eucharist? His words are here; his action of laying down his life in love for us is here; he shines in the faces of those who gather in his name; his acts of blessing, thanksgiving, and healing are here; his cross and resurrection are here in the breaking of the bread. The Eucharist is the greatest sign we have of what Christ is to us. Let us be aware that at any Eucharist, chances are non-Catholics are present. Aware of these guests in our midst, let us put on our best: be welcoming, be friendly, be receptive, be thankful, and be bread for the world.

CYCLE C

Genesis 14:18–20 Melchizedek brought bread and wine.

1 Corinthians 11:23–26 Every time you eat this bread and drink this cup, you are proclaiming the death of the Lord.

Luke 9:11–17 They all ate and were filled.

The Eucharist attracts most people to the Catholic Church. It is probably the most important element in your own faith life. Therefore it is a key means of evangelization. Although in the early church the Eucharistic ceremony was restricted to the faithful, today anyone may attend. There is a good chance that on any given Sunday, and especially on holidays, there will be a number of people who are not Catholic in attendance.

This is especially true at weddings, funerals, and baptisms. Given this situation, what can we as a Catholic community do to make non-Catholics feel comfortable and welcomed at our eucharistic celebrations? We may acknowledge their presence and verbally extend our welcome. We might have cards that they can sign that provide the opportunity to ask questions and to take advantage of any welcome programs we have in the parish. We may want to design booklets for non-Catholics that offer explanations of the parts of the Mass. How does our eucharistic community extend an invitation to non-Catholics to get to know us better? How do we and can we reach out to non-Catholics who may come to our services so that they feel welcomed and appreciated?

5

ORDINARY TIME

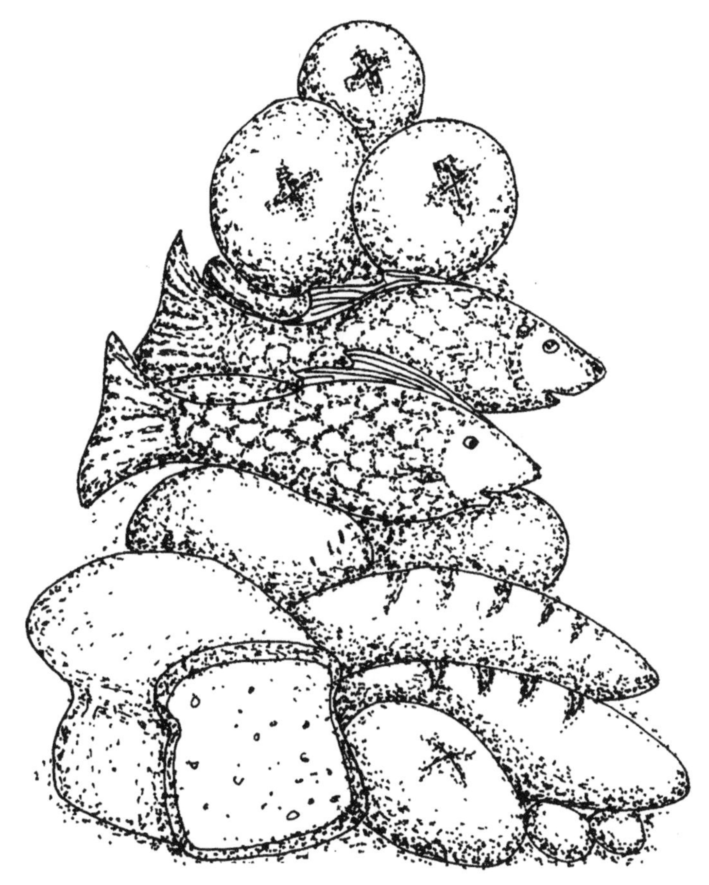

Second Sunday of the Year

CYCLE A

Isaiah 49:3, 5–6 I will make you the light of nations so that my salvation may reach the end of the earth.

1 Corinthians 1:13 The grace and peace of God our Father, and the Lord Jesus Christ be with you.

John 1:29–34 This is the Lamb of God that takes away the sins of the world.

The testimony of John the Baptist today is a wonderful example of evangelization. John attracts people through his message, charisma, and reputation. Yet John points beyond himself to Jesus. He does not stand in the way of Jesus. Instead he uses all his talents to draw people to himself so that he may more clearly point the way onward to Christ.

We can identify with John. We hope that people are attracted to us as persons and as a community because they sense something of the truth in us, something that draws and nourishes them. They sense something they want for themselves. Like John, we as a Christian community meet these people and minister to them. But we always, like John, point beyond ourselves to the one who is the true light. John says that he himself did not know Jesus. And we can say that as well. We are all of us ignorant of Jesus. As we go through life and our spiritual journeys, we hope that we come to know him better, but he will always be a mystery. There is more about him that we do not know than we do know. Yet in spite of this ignorance, our lives are centered around him: "...but I came baptizing for this reason—that he might be shown to Israel." We live our lives as witnesses so that others may come to know Jesus for themselves. And as they come to know and see Jesus, we, like John the Baptist, withdraw into the background. We have introduced them to the bridegroom, and we now step back so they may enter into union with him directly. Evangelization combines an active role—shining forth with the love and light of Christ so that others may come to know him—and then a passive role—stepping back or out of the way so that people might form their own appreciation of Jesus and his significance for them.

CYCLE B

1 Samuel 3:3–10, 19 Speak, Lord, your servant is listening.

1 Corinthians 6:13–15, 17–20 Your bodies are members of the body of Christ.

John 1:35–42 They saw where Jesus lived and they stayed with him.

The second reading speaks of the holiness of our bodies. Our bodies will be raised up. And truly "the Lord is for the body." Christians have traditionally honored the human body. It was necessary to keep to a middle path between divinizing the body and despising it. Our own culture makes the body divine and at the same time despises it. On the one hand we prize youthful looks excessively. Beautiful people are taken at face value, while those not considered gorgeous are ignored or passed over. As Christians we might convince our fellow citizens to value the spirit and what is within the person rather than the packaging. Our culture is youth obsessed; we often neglect the elderly, who are the repository of wisdom and experience. How do we as a community reserve a place of honor for the elderly?

On the other hand, our culture in many ways despises the body. We feed it junk food. We nourish addictions such as cigarettes, alcohol, and drugs, which harm the body. How do we individually and as a people show respect and love for our bodies, not because the body is who we are but because our bodies are for the Lord?

CYCLE C

Isaiah 62:1–5 As the bridegroom rejoices in his bride, so will your God rejoice in you.

1 Corinthians 12:4–11 One and the same Spirit distributes different gifts as he chooses.

John 2:1–12 The first of the signs given by Jesus was at Cana in Galilee.

The Wedding at Cana is the third shining forth of God's light commemorated in the feast of Epiphany. Jesus reveals God's glory by changing water into wine. Understand this story as an image for our world. Whether we know it or not, we are all at a wedding banquet. The prophets and Jesus himself frequently describe the kingdom of God as a wedding celebration: a celebration of God's abundance and goodness, and of God's love for us. God has invited us into a sacred covenant in Jesus. God has taken all of creation as bride.

In the story, everyone certainly knows that they are at a wedding feast. But they are unaware there is a crisis; the wine is running out. Mary knows this and immediately approaches Jesus. She models the way of a disciple. Our baptism and God's revelation make us privy to how things are really going at the feast. When we sense something wrong, we are encouraged to take this immediately to God. We are not supposed to try to correct it, but rather to bring it to God, surrender it, and be obedient, just as Mary tells the servants.

But there is a further commission. Only the disciples know what has happened. The host knows something has happened but gets it all wrong. We Christians also know what has happened in this world to make it so rich and wonderful. The Christ is present among us. It is up to us to share with everyone else the secret of this great marriage feast. The wine, this life, is wonderful and abundant because of Jesus' presence. How has he transformed your life? How is he transforming your neighbor's life? Can we share with one another the secret of what is happening in our midst?

Third Sunday of the Year

CYCLE A

Isaiah 8:23– 9:3 In the Galilean country, the people have seen a great light.

1 Corinthians 1:10–14,17 I appeal to you, my brothers and sisters, make up the difference between you.

Matthew 4:12–23 He went to Capernaum, that the prophecy of Isaiah be fulfilled.

One of the most common responses to the call to be evangelizers is that we are not ready, prepared, or worthy. That may be true, but worthiness is not part of the gospel demand. Indeed to be aware of our frailties and weaknesses is a key dimension of our spiritual journey. It helps us stay humble, with our feet on the ground. In the second reading, Paul berates the Corinthians over conflicts and fights within their community. Although this is not an ideal situation, it gives solace to know that our church has been human from the very beginning. These people were no holier than we are. And God takes them with all their faults and shortcomings to present the good news.

Paul hints that too much human proficiency may not be a good thing. He does not want to preach with such eloquence that the cross of Christ seems emptied of its power. When we present the gospel, we are not presenting ourselves, but someone who shines through us. Nor can the gospel be conveniently packaged: a cross has rough edges. It is not necessary for us to argue the gospel or win people over with our brilliance. It is enough that we share how the cross illumines our lives and community. This, as Paul says, will sound like foolishness to some, but to those who are open and receptive, the cross carries the power of God.

The gospel speaks of the sudden invitation to come follow Jesus and become fishers of people. The call may come out of the blue. Of course we do not feel ready or prepared. Yet we have the experience of Christ in our lives. We listen to God's word and are nourished at God's table. It is enough. If we stammer or stutter, people will hear the good news as long as the cross is present.

CYCLE B

Jonah 3:1–5, 10 The Ninevites renounced their evil ways.

1 Corinthians 7:29–31 The world as we know it is passing away.

Mark 1:14–20 Repent, and believe the Good news.

Jonah is a wonderful image for the evangelizer to contemplate. He is the reluctant prophet. He does not want to carry God's message to the Ninevites, and when he finally does, he is dumbfounded because these people whom he believed so godless heed the prophetic message and take it to heart unlike the Israelites, God's chosen ones. Jonah is reluctant first because he does not believe Nineveh deserves a chance to repent. Then he is flabbergasted when they do repent in a way that exceeds Israel's contrition.

We all have prejudices. Perhaps we feel deep down that non-Christians just are not good enough. Maybe we hope we might bring them into our light and so save them from themselves. But we might discover, like Jonah, that these so called "godless" people are more open to God and God's word than some Christians.

We need to look into our own hearts as well. Are we as open to God and God's presence as we might be? Do we take the gospel for granted, since we have been Christians for some time? Can we put ourselves, like the Ninevites, before the Word of God as though we had not heard it already and can we like them receive it into our hearts and act upon it?

CYCLE C

Nehemiah 8:2–4, 5–6, 8–10 They read from the book of Law and they understood what was read.

1 Corinthians 12:12–30 Together you are Christ's body, but each of you is a different part of it.

Luke 1:1–4; 4:14–21 The scriptures were fulfilled on this day.

Jesus goes to the synagogue, reads from the scroll of Isaiah, and announces that today this prophecy has come to pass. The prophecy is fulfilled in Jesus, and it continues to be fulfilled in his church. We have received the mission to bring glad tidings to the poor, sight to the blind, release to prisoners.

How do we do this in our community? Do we make a place for prisoners to alcohol and drugs? Is our church used only for services, or is it a beacon to the community for the poor, the blind, the imprisoned? What concrete things can we undertake that help us more clearly fulfill this prophecy of Christ's presence in our midst?

Fourth Sunday of the Year

CYCLE A

Zephaniah 2:3; 3:12–13 In your midst I will leave a humble and holy people.

1 Corinthians 1:26–31 God has chosen what is weak by human reckoning.

Matthew 5:1–12 Happy are the poor in spirit.

The second reading continues to speak of our call. There is nothing about us that makes us worthy of this call to preach the gospel. Unlike these Corinthians, we probably have wise, powerful, and influential people within our community. Yet they and the rest of us are not called because of that. And we show forth Christ most clearly not where we are strong but precisely where we are weak and deficient. As Paul says, God chose the foolish of this world to shame the wise, the weak to show up the strong.

Ask yourself whether you find God most present in your strengths and talents or where you are weak or unknowing. Again we are present in the mystery of the cross, where everything is turned upside down. On the cross, the Creator of the universe dies as a weak mortal. In doing so he overcomes all the powers of this world, including death. So in our lives and community, we find God in those places where we most need the help of a higher power. If we can do it on our own, why do we need God? Vulnerability therefore is a value of the evangelist. We do not need to have all the answers.

In fact, if we think we do, we probably are a hindrance in bringing people to the gospel. How do you feel when you are confronted by someone who seems to know it all? Do you become suspicious? Is this too good to be true? We do not have the answers; we do not know it all. What we have been given is a mystery—the cross. And within that mystery we grow in faith and trust that God is working God's way within us for the benefit of all God's creation.

CYCLE B

Deuteronomy 18:15–20 I will put my words into the prophet's mouth and he will tell them all I command.

1 Corinthians 7:32–35 The unmarried woman dedicates herself to the things of the Lord, that she might be holy

Mark 1:21–28 This is a new kind of teaching that speaks with authority.

We might ask ourselves what it means in our day to "speak with authority." The authority by which he spoke and behaved among them drew these first listeners to Jesus and his message. We may be tempted to look to the institutional church when we evangelize, but that will not do much good if the people to whom we are speaking are not already believers. On the other hand, we may share church teachings, such as those on social justice, that may appeal to contemporary people. If they see an institution that stands up for the individual person against all oppressive structures and institutions, an institution that seeks in every way to promote peace and an equitable distribution of the world's resources, they may recognize the voice of authority (the voice of truth) and be drawn to examine our faith more closely.

Often Jesus appeals to what we might call the authority of everyday life. "Who among you would give your child a stone if they asked for bread? Is not your heavenly Father more generous than that?" He appeals to the authority of our common experience.

We would do well to follow his example. How do you sense the mystery of God in your everyday life? Can you locate God's presence in experiences shared by all human beings?

In the gospel, the evil spirits that have possessed the man identify Jesus as the Holy One of God. Do the voices of oppression and evil in our society recognize us and the church as the agents of a loving and merciful God? Is our voice heard against war and violence? Are our actions in solidarity with the poor and the outcast? We may not be on the winning side, but are we witnessing to the Holy One of God?

CYCLE C

Jeremiah 1:4–5, 17–19 I have appointed you as a prophet to the nations.

1 Corinthians 12:31–13:13 There are three things that last: faith, hope and love; and the greatest of these is love.

Luke 4:21–30 No prophet is accepted in his own country.

Today's gospel concludes the story begun last Sunday. There Jesus announced that the prophecy had been fulfilled. But he goes on to say that those present are not to share in it. In reaction the crowd tries to kill him. Jesus never appears without the cross, without the crisis that he brings us. This crisis reveals how far we are from God's righteousness. We must be willing to look at our own shortcomings, as well as those of our culture and society. We Americans like to consider ourselves God's chosen people, but do we act accordingly? Are we a people of peace? Do we care for the orphan, the widow, the poor? Do we release captives, or build better prisons?

God's word stands in judgment over us and our culture. But it is not a word that merely condemns. In that case we could only despair. No, it is a word that leads to life. The people try to kill Jesus, as they will later succeed in doing.

But God's response now as then is to bring forth life. Jesus escapes the crowd now as later he will escape the tomb. God speaks not to damn us but to show the way to true life. We are witnesses to that Word. We are God's voice for the poor, the blind, the imprisoned.

Fifth Sunday of the Year

CYCLE A

Isaiah 58:7–10 Your light will shine like the dawn.

1 Corinthians 2:1–5 I have told you of the witness of the crucified Christ.

Matthew 5:13–16 You are the light of the world.

Isaiah stresses evangelization as action. We will make our God known by our works: feeding the hungry, sheltering the homeless. When we do these things we show forth the God we believe in. For God above all is merciful and cares for all creatures, especially for the poor.

Paul speaks of his weakness as a part of his preaching the gospel. God makes use of our weakness as well.

God chooses us in all our many facets, including our weaknesses. We cannot excuse ourselves from being signs of evangelization because we do not know enough, or we are not good enough. God's wisdom shines forth precisely through our weakness.

Jesus tells us the true end of evangelization. We are to be signs of God's love and goodness. Evangelization is not about converting people or getting more members for the church; that is a by product. We are called first and foremost to be a light for others by which they might come to know our God.

CYCLE B

Job 7:1–4,6–7 I am filled with sorrows all day long.

1 Corinthians 9:16–19,22–23 Punishment will come to me if I do not preach the gospel.

Mark 1:29–39 He cured many who suffered from diseases of one kind or another.

Many people today echo Job's lament. They are sick, addicted, without employment or purpose in this world. This is the human condition. The Buddha spoke of life as inherently unsatisfactory. True, when our life is going well we can deceive ourselves and believe all is well, but death waits for each and every one of us.

Jesus incarnates God's response to our human condition. He reaches out as in today's gospel to cure our ills. And if we would continue his ministry as he has called us to do, we too must reach out with compassion and hope to those who suffer. While we may be able to reach out only a little on our own, we are not solitary; we are a community called "church."

We discover the power and ability to reach out as did Jesus: through prayer. Repeatedly throughout his ministry he would withdraw into prayer. Without a good prayer life—both individual and communal—we will not be able to take on this ministry of evangelization. Whenever you begin to feel overwhelmed by your ministry, whether individually or as a parish group, understand that as a sign to withdraw into prayer until you are refreshed and reinvigorated. Trust in God to sustain this great ministry we have been given; God will provide.

Finally, notice that when Jesus comes out of prayer he does not go back to the same group. He moves onward and outward. Paul talks about being under compulsion to preach the gospel. The missionary is like the sower scattering seeds. Do not focus on just one thing all the time. Try various means and methods of evangelization. Go to different groups and peoples. Spread yourself wide. We may never know what will happen to the seeds we sow, but, like Paul, we hope to share in its blessings.

CYCLE C

Isaiah 6:1–2, 3–8 Here am I! Send me.

1 Corinthians 15:1–11 I preach what they preach, and this is what you believe.

Luke 5:1–11 They left everything and followed him.

The first reading and the gospel focus upon God's call. This summons begins our spiritual journey. Each one of us has received this call from God to be bearers of God's good news. The call does not happen as dramatically as with Isaiah or as obviously as with Simon, but it is present nevertheless. It came to us through the community that baptized and received us into it, promising to oversee our growth in the Spirit.

Perhaps we pretend we have not really been called. The call only comes to the professionals: the priests and religious who have received a vocation to the ministry or religious life. We do not speak of our life as a call unless we think of the vocation to marriage. But the call is there nevertheless. We may try to avoid it by saying that we are not yet ready. But the call comes now. It is present today. Jesus calls Peter in the midst of his work as a fisherman. God does not wait until we are ready. God can use us here and now.

Our response when we realize the call echoes Simon Peter: "Lord, I am a sinful man." We do and should feel inadequate when we realize God is calling us. It is a humbling experience. But our humility is part of the call. Yes, we, each one of us, are given the gift of being fishers of people: we are all evangelists.

Sixth Sunday of the Year

CYCLE A

Sirach 15:15–20 He never commanded anyone to be godless.

1 Corinthians 2:6–10 God in his wisdom predestined our glory before the ages began.

Matthew 5:17–37 Such was said to your ancestors; but I am speaking to you.

We are to be signs of God to the world. The Sermon on the Mount shows us how we must conform ourselves to God so that the world may recognize God in our actions. This is not a new list of laws but rather a vision that draws us ever onward in holiness. Our sanctity will provide others a glimpse of our God. We are to be a people of peace. Let us not only refrain from killing but even seek to cast out anger. Only if we continually reach for the vision Jesus offers will we be able to evangelize. How can we make this vision of life attractive to others? How does it challenge us to continue growing in holiness?

Jesus' injunctions go against what we consider our human nature. It is hard if not impossible to drop our anger, our lust, our sense of self-importance. And we will often feel this advice is downright stupid when wrestling with our instincts. Yet in these injunctions, which look like folly in the world's eyes, is hidden the wisdom of God that Paul mentions. The gospel opposes the world. God does not ask us to go with the flow. God calls us to change. Within that change is wisdom.

Today the Catholic Church is one of the few voices against divorce. Marriage is difficult especially when we can expect it to last thirty to forty years. Our culture claims that if the relationship becomes difficult it is not right for you: get a divorce. Our teaching says that if the relationship becomes difficult, then the couple is called to further conversion together. No one is completely compatible with anyone else. In a continuing relationship, we must die to ourselves as individuals and become a new couple. A stable marriage in which both people continue to work on their relationship is a wonderful evangelizing sign to our culture. Our commitment to marriage reveals the richness of life that such a sacrament can bring.

CYCLE B

Leviticus 13:1–2, 44–46 As long as he is unclean, he must live alone, outside the camp.

1 Corinthians 10:31–11:1 Be imitators of me, as I am of Christ.

Mark 1:40–45 He sent the leper from him and he was cured.

Leviticus speaks of how lepers should be treated. They must be kept isolated from the larger society so that others are not infected. Consider our modern lepers. Whom do we regard as unclean? Gays and lesbians? Persons with AIDS? The divorced? The mentally ill? Addicts and alcoholics? Child abusers?

Jesus does not reject lepers. He heals them. He welcomes them into his presence and returns them to community. In his eyes no one is excluded. How do we live out this way of healing in our Christian community? Do we provide a welcome to those excluded elsewhere? Do we hold out the hand of compassion?

Let us not deceive ourselves. Often it takes no miraculous power to heal someone; all it takes is the compassion and welcome of a community. We may not be able to cure people with AIDS, but we can bring them Christ's healing power, which acquaints them with God's love as they experience it through our church.

Finally, Paul reminds us that whatever we do should be accomplished so that the glory of God might shine forth. We are not here to give offense to others, but to embody God's compassion and desire to draw all people together in peaceful fellowship. Let us examine our lives as individuals as well as church. How does each of our actions manifest the glory of God? How might we express that glory even more luminously in our personal lives and in our church?

CYCLE C

Jeremiah 17:5–8 Unhappy is he who trusts in man; happy the man who trusts in the Lord.

1 Corinthians 15:12, 16–20 If Christ is not raised from the dead, your faith is in vain.

Luke 6:17, 20–26 Happy are the poor; their reward will be great.

Today's gospel, the beginning of the Sermon on the Plain, contains the core of the good news with which we are entrusted. Jesus speaks good news to the poor: theirs is the kingdom of God. He turns our ordinary perceptions on their heads. The poor have the kingdom; the rich are rejected. We are blessed when people hate us; we are in trouble when we are satiated.

Paul in the second reading describes the most paradoxical event we must witness: a dead man has been raised to life. We live in a culture of death; Christians must proclaim a word of life and resurrection in the midst of this death. Like the Beatitudes, this message sounds foolish to the wisdom of this world. But as Paul says, if Christ does not live, we are all dead.

In this topsy-turvy world that appears to be coming apart at the seams, perhaps only a gospel of the ostensibly absurd can break through and save us. As Jeremiah vouches, we have trusted in human beings for most of our history. In God's eyes such trust is a curse. We are challenged today to trust in the Lord, to have our hope in this ridiculous Lord of the poor, the persecuted, the meek, the hungry. Only such faith brings life and allows us to grow like the wonderful tree Jeremiah pictures.

Seventh Sunday of the Year

CYCLE A

Leviticus 19:1–2, 17–18 You must love your neighbor, as yourself.

1 Corinthians 3:16–23 All things are yours, but you belong to Christ and Christ belongs to God.

Matthew 5:38–48 Love your enemies.

Both Leviticus and Jesus make love a key point of evangelization. We are people loved by God, and we in turn love our neighbors. We must be a loving community. We must love one another. And our love must extend to all those not part of our immediate community. In such love we experience God. In such love others will be able to experience God.

Of course it is easier to talk about love than actually to love. Love takes lots of work. It demands everything of us. Even if we are in love with a person, there will be times when we do not love him or her. Or at least there are times when we do not like the other person. How much more difficult then is love within the larger Christian community? Any parish has people whom we find it hard to love. They get on our nerves; we may disagree about different things; we see things in diverse ways. The command to love demands that we overcome these differences. We won't be condemned for failing, only for not trying. And whenever we are able to show forth such love, we manifest God's presence.

CYCLE B

Isaiah 43:18–19, 21–22, 24–25 On account of me your iniquities are blotted out.

2 Corinthians 1:18–22 Every promise of God finds its affirmative in Jesus.

Mark 2:1–12 The Son of Man has authority on earth to forgive sins.

Notice how Jesus sets up the circumstances in today's gospel. This could be a simple healing story. A lame man appeals to him and he responds with God's healing touch. But instead Jesus turns it into a teaching for all present.

He responds at first not with healing, but with forgiveness. He purposefully means to antagonize the scribes: only God can forgive sins. Who is this man?

When they challenge him Jesus responds, "Which is easier, to forgive sins or heal a cripple?" The theological rejoinder is of course that healing is easier since only God can forgive sins. But the common sense answer knows that forgiving sins is easier since no one knows whether this has really occurred. If you ask someone to walk, your ability is clearly exhibited.

In our own efforts at evangelization, our actions and deeds will speak much more loudly and clearly than our words alone. It is easy to say, "Let's take care of the poor and outcast." But it is an infinitely more powerful witness to actually do this. And we need not do it on our own. We are part of a worldwide community of faith. Actually we are unable do this work alone, but together we can provide a powerful witness on behalf of God's saving power to our neighbors and our culture.

Isaiah says God is doing something new, and Paul speaks of Jesus as the eternal "Yes" of God. This "new something" did not end in Jesus nor did the "Yes." Today through us God continues doing something new and wonderful. Presently God still speaks an unequivocal "Yes" to every human being. How do we and can we join in this wonderful happening? How can we put the resources of our church at the service of the forgiveness of sins and the healing of the lame in our own day?

CYCLE C

1 Samuel 26:2, 7–9, 12–13, 22–23 The Lord has put you in my power, but I will not raise my hand against you.

1 Corinthians 15:45–49 Just as we have carried the earthly image, we must carry the heavenly image.

Luke 6:27–38 Be merciful as your Father is merciful.

The gospel today continues preaching the good news of salvation. We are to love our enemies, turn the other cheek, give to all who ask. These are easy words to speak, but our evangelization must include more than words. We are asked to conform our lives to these ideas.

How does our community show its love for all people and treat supposed enemies as friends? Are there people whom we regard as enemies? How might we befriend them? Do we regularly pray for those who oppose us? How do we pray? Do we ask for their undoing? Do we ask that they be converted to our way? Or do we honestly pray for their good?

In the second reading, Paul speaks of the spiritual emerging from the earthly. We might apply this teaching to the gospel today. It is normal to hate one's enemies, common to revenge wrongdoing against us. This is normal to our humanity. But the gospel calls us to the spiritual. We are challenged to evolve beyond what is natural. Only in the spiritual can we find happiness and wholeness. While it may seem we are going against the grain when we try to follow Jesus' teachings, we are truly advancing toward our own as well as everyone else's happiness.

Eighth Sunday of the Year

CYCLE A

Isaiah 49:14–15 Even these may forget, says the Lord, yet I will not forget you.

1 Corinthians 4:1–5 The Lord will bring light to all that is hidden in darkness.

Matthew 6:24–34 Do not worry about your life and what you are to eat or to wear.

The content of our evangelization does not always have to be the person of Jesus. His message is just as important and will help people even if they do not come to the fullness of faith. As we see from the first reading, Jesus' teaching about God is not unique to him but comes out of the Hebraic tradition. What a powerful image: Even if a mother should forget her child, God will not forget or forsake us. We know the strength of the bond between mother and child. The child is from her flesh, and she nourishes it with her milk. Yet our bond with God is stronger yet. It is very easy to feel alone and forsaken in our world. This message provides hope for us all. God is and will always be with us.

In the second reading, Paul talks about standing outside of judgment. The world runs on judgment. From the time we are born till the time we die we are being judged. And we quickly learn to judge ourselves as well as others. We continually compare ourselves to some standard—usually an impossibly high one. Yet Paul encourages us to drop the judgments both against ourselves and against others. To forsake judgment allows us to live in a realm of freedom and peace. Imagine what it is like to have nothing on one's conscience. Isn't that possibility the best of good news?

In the gospel, Jesus advises us to let go of worry. It doesn't do any good and yet it consumes lots of time. What would your life be like if you could let go of just a little of your present worry? These teachings are the very core of the gospel. They are the good news we have to tell. How can we proclaim this in our lives and in our actions?

CYCLE B

Hosea 2:16–17, 21–22 I will betroth you to me for ever.

2 Corinthians 3:1–6 You are a letter from Christ for us to deliver.

Mark 2:18–22 The bridegroom is still with them.

Paul instructs the Corinthians that they are his letter of recommendation. They are Christ's letter written by the Spirit on hearts of flesh. So as we consider evangelization we realize that we ourselves are first and foremost God's signs in the world. We are the Spirit's letter sent to today's people proclaiming the good news of God's love in Jesus Christ. What is important is not so much our preaching as our living. How can people read this letter clearly from our lives and the actions of our church within our local community?

The faithful and sacrificing love of a married couple is one of the clearest signs of God's love. Hosea uses the image of romance to speak of God's relationship to us. And Jesus seizes upon the figure of the bridegroom to speak of himself.

Many of us are living the sacrament of matrimony. This sacrament is not merely for the benefit of the couple. Yes, we find within it the love of God manifested in our love for our spouse and their love for us. But we are also a sign of God's love to others. How is our family a manifestation of forgiving and compassionate love? Is our home a place of welcome to others? As a family do we reach out to include others in our lives? Or do we close in on ourselves? Are there family secrets that keep us from encountering the freeing power of love? How might spouses grow more deeply in love with one another and in doing so with God? And how might that love radiate outwards to other members of the church and of our neighborhood?

CYCLE C

Sirach 27:4–7 Do not praise a man before he has spoken.
1 Corinthians 15:54–58 Victory has been given us through Jesus Christ.
Luke 6:39–45 A man speaks from what is in his heart.

In the gospel, Jesus urges the need for conversion in order to undertake the ministry of an evangelist. What good does it do if we ourselves do not live our message? A major difference between Catholic and fundamentalist Christians lies in our different appreciations of conversion. For Catholics, conversion is not a one-time thing. Responding to the call of Jesus inaugurates a lifetime journey of conversion. In our evangelization we constantly need to listen ourselves to the gospel message and allow that message to transform our lives and community. We are not saints; we are a people in transition, a pilgrim people, a populace continually in need of and hopefully always open to conversion.

If our message is of social justice, we need to ask how we too in our church and in our lives can be more just. Are we continually willing to change in the same way that the gospel invites all to grow? We are not people who have the truth and then seek to bring that truth to others. That same truth challenges us, reveals our sinfulness, calls us to perfection as much as it does the world.

Unfortunately the church sometimes gives the impression that she is perfect and judges others as less so. But we are not above the message we bring. We too, even more than nonbelievers, are called to conversion by this good news. We are not exempt. We cannot demand from the world an end to discrimination when we practice it internally. There is not one truth for the church and another for the world. There is only one gospel.

As evangelists, we are exhorted to bring forth good fruit. In the end we shall be known by our fruits. As Chesterton said, it is not that Christianity has been tried and found wanting; it is that Christianity has been found difficult and seldom tried. In evangelization God wishes us to live rather than simply speak the gospel.

We will not be judged for failing to live up to the high standards of the good news. We will only be judged for failing even to try. As Paul reminds us, we already have assurance of the victory in Jesus Christ. Death is already swallowed up in the resurrection. So we can afford to risk everything by allowing the gospel to penetrate and convert our lives and church. Christ has already won the victory for us. If we are joined with him in the great ministry of evangelization, that victory can never be snatched from us.

Ninth Sunday of the Year

CYCLE A

Deuteronomy 11:18, 26–28, 32 I set before you today a blessing and a curse.

Romans 3:21–25,28 A person is justified by his faith, not by law.

Matthew 7:21–27 A wise person builds their house on rock, not on sand.

We could read today's lessons in order as a presentation of the good news. From Deuteronomy, we hear the proclamation of the Law. We are told to take it into our hearts and obey it. But as Paul, a righteous Jew, has discovered, it is impossible for a human being to live up to the Law in its fullness. Only people who do not look closely at the Law and at their own lives can deceive themselves into believing they are following the Law.

The good news we receive in the gift of Jesus Christ declares that we are undeservedly justified. Jesus restores us to full communion with God. Indeed we are now God's own children. We are not doomed to the futility of trying to fulfill the Law and achieve a humanly impossible standard.

So does this gift free us from all responsibility? No. If we truly accept the grace of Jesus we will be transformed. We will fulfill the Law not under our own will but through the will of God and of Jesus Christ. It is all too easy to claim Jesus as a savior and let it go at that. But Jesus' own words tell us that it is not what we say but how we live that reveals who we are. We will not be condemned because we have fallen short of the gospel or the Law. We will only be lost because we did not risk even trying to walk in the way of truth and life. Our lives are our first witness to the world. Our words simply follow our deeds. Such is true evangelization.

CYCLE B

Deuteronomy 5:12–15 Remember that you were a servant in the land of Egypt and that the Lord God brought you out.

2 Corinthians 4:6–11 The life of Jesus is revealed in our body.

Mark 2:23–36 The Son of Man is master even of the sabbath.

For us the first reading is likely to be more shocking than the gospel. Our culture has certainly succeeded in making the Sabbath (or the Lord's Day) agreeable to human beings. We are far from Jerusalem, where the siren sounds at Sabbath sundown and all traffic and commerce ceases for a day. Our own keeping of the Sabbath may be limited to attending Mass. But is the entire day one of rest and relaxation with your family? Or is it filled with things that didn't get done during the rest of the week?

For Israel, the Sabbath was a sign of God's covenant as much as the mark of circumcision. And for Christians, although we moved the celebration from Saturday to the first day of the week in honor of the resurrection, the Sabbath rest was observed until recently.

We are a culture in furious motion. Most stores are open seven days a week. If we desire we can treat each day as equal to any other. And advertising and the mass media certainly encourage us to consume without end.

But does such a rat-race existence provide peace and happiness? What might it be like to reserve one day weekly for the truly important things in life? What are these? Worship of God, key human relationships, play, prayer, and relaxation. Do we make time to appreciate God in nature? Do we walk in the woods? Do we plant gardens and nourish them? Do we play with our children, read to them, listen to them, educate them in the pleasures of a full life?

We certainly do not want to return to a rigid observance of Sabbath, where our own well-being might be sacrificed to a law. Jesus frees us from that and puts things in proper perspective: The Sabbath was made for us, not we for the Sabbath. God gives us this wonderful gift. Do we make use of it? Can others see in our Sabbath observances signs of our values and priorities? Or are we just like our neighbors saving that we cram one hour of church into our already crowded schedule?

CYCLE C

1 Kings 8:41–43 When the stranger comes, hear him.

Galatians 1:1–2,6–10 If I tried to please man, I could not be a servant of Christ.

Luke 7:1–10 Nowhere in Israel have I found as much faith.

Today's readings highlight a tension we must always preserve as proclaimers of the good news. On the one hand, Paul warns us to preserve the gospel from being distorted for whatever reason—to win approval, or to make it more palatable. What is that good news but the offer of healing and wholeness as a pure gift through the cross of Jesus Christ? By whatever means we proclaim the good news, we should be leading people toward Jesus—the message and the man. We may do so in contemporary language and with contemporary forms of thought, but however we couch our message it must center on the grace poured out on the world through this man and his voluntary sacrifice of his life for us.

However, this grace does not come upon us only when we acknowledge and put our faith in Jesus. God's

Spirit is not restricted to Christians alone. It is available to all. When people come to us we ought to be open to seeing how grace is already leavening their lives.

We can share with them our own experience of grace—the stories of scripture and of our life. But we also descry the good news in the stories they tell us. So in today's gospel we see the faith of the Roman centurion is more powerful than most Israelites. The centurion has experienced God's love. This love draws him to Jesus, whom he senses is a vehicle for that love and healing. He is coming to acknowledge Jesus as God's human form in the world. He is beginning to put Jesus at the center of his life—the person in whom he beholds God's power manifesting in the world.

Solomon is aware that the temple is not simply for Israel, but will become a place for all peoples to worship God. They will be drawn by their own appreciation of God operative in their own lives and cultures. Solomon asks us to listen to them. They have something to teach us. Evangelization is not a one-way street. When people approach us, they come because they have already met God. They have discerned the divine. If we honor their ways, we too will encounter new facets of God's grace.

Today Christians dialogue with other religions. We do so not to save them. They are already saved by the power of God, which we identify as centered in Jesus Christ—the pure gospel that Paul admonishes us to keep uncontaminated. Through our dialogue we may aid them to find a closer relationship with God, and we may find through their experience paths that lead us ever deeper into the mystery that can never be fully understood: God's infinite compassion and grace.

Through Christian-Buddhist dialogue, the many ways of meditation and contemplation, ignored and forgotten parts of the Christian tradition, have been restored to a multitude of people. Our friendship with Buddhists has renewed Christian spirituality and opened to ordinary Catholics paths by which they may approach the mystery of God and be converted by that meeting.

We do not give up our own gospel. But what that gospel offers our Buddhist brothers and sisters can only be witnessed to by them. Our purpose is not to convert them but that all might come closer to the temple of God's glory at the heart of all true spiritual traditions.

Tenth Sunday of the Year

CYCLE A

Hosea 6:3–6 What I want is love, not sacrifice, says the Lord.

Romans 4:18–25 He drew strength from his faith while giving glory to God.

Matthew 9:9–13 I did not come to call the just, but sinners.

Hosea presents a powerful revelation of God. First, God is frustrated with us. How slow we are to approach the truth! We avoid the life God offers us. We cover it over with piety; we pretend to respond to God by offering sacrifices and other religious works. Yet God truly wants not lip service, but a relationship with us. God desires that we reciprocate God's love. God wants us to get to know God like a close friend. God wants to enter into a relationship with us.

This invitation to enter into a relationship of love is the heart of revelation. Once we enter more deeply into our own relationship with God, then we can extend the invitation to others to come to know God by asking them to participate in our own friendship with God.

Paul tells us how much this relationship depends upon faith. Faith is not knowledge of religious truths. It is a relationship of trust. Abraham trusted that the promises he and Sarah received would be fulfilled even though they seemed absurd. So for us to make spiritual progress we too must learn to trust God's will for us. Our true happiness is found only in God's will.

In the gospel, we can see that love as well as that trust at work. Matthew is a tax collector—an enemy of his own people, a collaborator with the Roman oppressors. Yet Jesus calls out to him. Matthew senses the love in that call, for he leaves everything from his old life behind and sets out to follow Jesus. He hears something in that call that leads him to trust this man.

What is the story of our faith? In what ways have we come to trust God and Jesus? And how has that faith led us deeper into the arms of our lover? This is the content of the good news that we can share with other Christians and the world.

CYCLE B

Genesis 3:9–15 I will make you enemies of each other; your offspring and her offspring.

2 Corinthians 4:13–5:1 We believe, and therefore we speak.

Mark 3:20–35 It is the end of Satan.

Paul says, "We believe and so we speak." Indeed, do we really believe if we do not speak out? Reflect on the times when you were in love. Could you keep silent about it? Faith is like love; when we truly believe we cannot help but give voice to it. And when we speak of our faith it is invigorated and deepened. Everything becomes ordered to our benefit. We are renewed in heart and able to witness to Christ and his kingdom.

As we witness we find we are drawn more fully into the family of Christ. As the gospel says, "Whoever does the will of God is brother, sister and mother to me." As faith is like love so it is also like family. We are part of a family and we draw strength and nourishment from the other members. Evangelization is not a solitary endeavor; it is a family affair. As we share faith with others, our own faith is deepened and renewed. On the other hand, if we keep our faith to ourselves it does not grow but shrivels up and dies. Only by giving away what we have are we strengthened and renewed.

CYCLE C

1 Kings 17:17–24 Look, said Elijah, your son is living.

Galatians 1:11–19 God has revealed his Son in me, that I might preach the good news about him to the pagans.

Luke 7:11–17 Young man, I say to you, arise.

Let's imagine ourselves as the apostles. We had known Jesus and we had participated in the full course of his arrest, crucifixion, and then resurrection. Now here comes this man who had been one of our chief persecutors. Out of the blue he tells us that he has met the Risen Lord. No one had shared the gospel with him. No one had instructed him. He has not gone through whatever catechumenate might have been in place to accompany people on their journey toward acceptance of the gospel. When he had his conversion experience he did not come to the Christian community to have it affirmed. Instead he went off to the desert by himself. And now he approaches Peter and James (or you) and tells you that he has been commissioned to work with non-Jews. As an evangelist, how would you respond to him?

It is easy in hindsight to affirm his ministry. After all this is Paul—the apostle to the Gentiles—the second most important figure in all Christianity. But look at how he comes to accept the good news. It is not through any contact with the church. Indeed very quickly he will challenge the pillars of the church over the practice of circumcision.

In our own evangelization we too must be open to the people whom we engage in dialogue. What do they have to share with us about Jesus and the gospel? Our own understanding and even the church's does not exhaust the depths of the gospel. The Holy Spirit cannot be contained nor the mystery of God's love depleted.

When we encounter the Holy Spirit outside our church walls, will we be ready and able to acknowledge its presence, as did Peter and James? Or will we resort to the safety of our traditions and snuff out the Spirit's voice because we cannot recognize God's signs, which continually surprise us and bring us new life?

Evangelization is a two-way street. We bring the good news to non-Christians; they in turn share their experience of the gospel with us. It takes courage and risk to do so. We will be changed. Our church will be changed. Look at what Paul brought to the faith! He made it possible for the gospel to become a world religion rather than a tiny sect of Judaism.

Eleventh Sunday of the Year

CYCLE A

Exodus 19:2–6 You will be a kingdom of priests, a consecrated nation.

Romans 5:6–11 We have been reconciled to God through the death of his Son; we are saved by his life.

Matthew 9:36–10:8 He summoned his twelve disciples, and sent them out.

Paul meditates upon God's great love for us. While we were still sinners God reached out in love to us: Christ died for us. How unthinkable this is! As Paul says, you are not likely to die for a good person let alone for someone who is unworthy. Yet this is just what God has done. We are all, every last one of us, reconciled in Christ. Now this is the real good news. Everyone is already reconciled in Christ. It does not depend upon becoming worthy of it; it does not depend upon straightening out our lives. It comes as a totally free gift from God.

Shouldn't everybody have the chance to hear this good news? This is exactly our ministry as evangelizers. We are here to deliver this gospel to people in whatever way possible, in the hope that they are able to hear it and come to rejoice with us in God through our Lord Jesus Christ. We proclaim the gospel through our words, through our actions, through our values, through our very lives.

CYCLE B

Exodus 17:22–24 I have made the small tree great.

2 Corinthians 5:6–10 Whether we are living in the body or exiled from it, we are intent on pleasing the Lord.

Mark 4:26–34 The mustard seed, the smallest of all the seeds, grows into the biggest shrub of all.

We could compare our faith to the mustard seed. Few of us believe that our faith is strong or full. Yet according to the parable, it need not be. It need only resemble a mustard seed. What are we to do with this mustard seed? We sow it. We do not need to take more classes, study more, pray more before we evangelize. In the act of evangelizing God will guide us, strengthen us, and increase our faith. Only by letting the seed fall on the ground does it have the opportunity to develop into the mustard bush.

Stay with this image of the mustard bush. It is a strange concept. We might think that Jesus would choose a more noble and grand representation (an oak, for example) to exemplify the kingdom of God. But instead he selects the mustard bush. It is not majestic, but it is quite useful. Mustard flavors our food. And the bush shelters the birds of the sky.

Our evangelization may not be noble and grand. We may not make a name for ourselves. We may not bring thousands of people to the knowledge of God. But we are doing something useful and necessary by our humble efforts. We are nourishing our community and others. We provide sanctuary for people by disclosing the love and mercy of God.

CYCLE C

2 Samuel 12:7–10,13 The Lord God forgave your sin; you will not die.

Galatians 2:16,19–21 I live now, not with my own life, but with the life of Christ who lives in me.

Luke 7:36–50 Her many sins were forgiven her, because she has shown great love.

David does not earn his place in sacred history through his virtue. He sinned grievously and often. What redeems him is his honesty and his quickness to seek God's forgiveness. Our God is not chiefly a lawyer but a reconciler. Remember this is the same God who takes on human form in Jesus.

Jesus too is much more interested in our reconciliation than he is in judging us. The penitent woman shocks the righteous people, but to Jesus she is closer to God than the others. The weight of her sins has been lifted, and she comes to bathe his feet.

Paul also affirms the gospel not as a law or set of rules to be obeyed, but rather as a trust in God's grace received through Jesus Christ. Paul likewise speaks of conversion. How he was crucified with Christ and now is risen in Christ. We are a new creation in Christ: this is the primary means of evangelization. Let us not hide what God has done for us. Let us boast of it. My life is not my own creation. It has been raised up for me, and God's grace now empowers me to live as I do.

Who we are speaks the gospel much more forcefully than any words. How do I manifest God's forgiveness in my life? How does our Christian community present the reality of forgiveness and reconciliation in our neighborhood? Is our church a place where all people know they are welcomed and have a home? Do we reach out to the alienated and forgotten?

Twelfth Sunday of the Year

CYCLE A

Jeremiah 20:10–13 He has delivered the soul of the needy from the hands of evil people.

Romans 5:12–15 God's gift to us is nothing like our sin against God.

Matthew 10:26–33 Do not fear those who can kill the body.

Jesus speaks to us today about our mission to share his good news. He asks us to proclaim it from the housetops. And he tells us not to be afraid of our message. There is no need for us to succeed in evangelizing. It is not up to us whether people listen to us or not. Perhaps they will not understand us. After all, a God who pulls life out of death or who takes flesh as an ordinary human being is rather strange news. Yet it provides us with life and hope. Now we are sent to share that hope with our brothers and sisters. We need not fear being misunderstood or even persecuted. As Jesus assures us, no one can separate us from God's love. All we need fear is the cowardice of not saying who we are and what we believe. To be a Christian is not to be saved. Everyone is saved in Jesus. To be a Christian is to know this good news and be willing to share it with others.

CYCLE B

Job 38:1,8–11 Here I have set the boundaries of the sea.

2 Corinthians 5:14–17 All things are made new.

Mark 4:35–41 Who can this be? Even the wind and the sea obey him.

Like the disciples we have suffered storms and squalls both in our private life and in our community.

And like the disciples we have weathered the storm. Our boat has not capsized. We were borne up by the power of Christ. We too can ask their question, "Who can this be that the wind and sea obey him?"

And what is our answer? Who is this man for us? Who do we deem him to be? It is not sufficient to repeat the traditional words and answers of faith. What has he revealed to us of God and Jesus? How has Jesus soothed the storms in our life? If we can tell that story in our own words, we, like the disciples, are proclaiming the good news.

As we grew to know Jesus better, we came to understand that, as Paul declares, Jesus calmed our storms by dying for us. After the tempest is settled we have sought to live not for ourselves but for him. But to accomplish that we must live as he did—for others.

What are the storms we see about us: in people's lives, in our society? How are people around us suffering? We see families tossed by the storms of modern life. How do we bring the peace and assurance of Christ's love to them? How can we become transparent so that Jesus through us might calm these tempests of the soul?

CYCLE C

Zechariah 12:10–11 They will look on the one whom they have pierced.

Galatians 3:26–29 You who have been baptized have put on Christ.

Luke 9:18–24 You're the Messiah sent by God. It is necessary for the Son of Man to suffer much.

"Who do people say that I am?" This is not even a question for us. We all know the answer. We wait for Peter to cough it up, "You are the Christ!" But what does this mean for us today? Peter and the apostles acknowledge

Jesus as the Messiah for whom Israel longed. But who is he for Americans today? It does not really mean much to tell a non-Jew that Jesus fulfilled the scriptures. So what? What makes those scriptures so special in the first place?

Let us take Jesus' question seriously. There is no pat answer today. Yes, he is the Christ, but what does that really mean? Who is Jesus for you? What does he mean to you? What does he demand of you? What does he do for you and for us? If we would bring the good news of Jesus to our world, we must do so couched in our own hopes, fears, and dreams.

The gospel stories are shaped by the Hebrew scriptures, which those first Christians considered inspired. When we tell the story of Jesus it must be set within the narrative of our own life and experience. Why is he so important to us? If we can tell that story, others will long to know him too. Jesus makes an impact on the people he meets—a significant impact. Those imprints lead the disciples to their confession. Who is he for us? Who is he for me and for you? Let us tell that story to one another and to the world.

Thirteenth Sunday of the Year

CYCLE A

2 Kings 4:8–11, 14–16 That is the holy man of God, let him remain there.

Romans 6:3–4, 8–11 Having been buried with him through baptism, we shall walk in a new life.

Matthew 10:37–42 Anyone who does not accept his cross is not worthy of me. Anyone who welcomes you, welcomes me.

Paul speaks of baptism as our participation in Christ's death and resurrection. Christians experience the resurrection at Easter in the conversion and baptism of catechumens. They are for us the dying and rising of Christ. And we too are signs of Christ to the world if we live this dying and rising in our own lives.

Our existence is filled with deaths: small deaths like graduation from school or moving from our home towns, larger deaths such as the death of a friendship or a marriage. And of course literal death: the death of friends and loved ones, and ultimately our own death. How do we face these deaths? Do we see them as ends or as new beginnings? Are they to be feared, or embraced because they open the possibility of new resurrections?

Our hope is grounded in Christ's rising from the dead. His resurrection announces that resurrection is possible from every death. If we face life's many deaths with this hope, we become powerful signs of the resurrection to our brothers and sisters; just as our catechumens inspire us by giving up their old lives to join our family.

CYCLE B

Wisdom 1:13–15; 2:23–24 It was the devil's envy that brought death into the world.

2 Corinthians 8:7, 9, 13–15 Your abundance should supply their want.

Mark 5:21–43 Young girl, I say to you, arise.

"Fear is useless. What is needed is trust." Does this strike you as good news? Our lives often run on fear. Our society employs fear to keep its constituents in line. It believes that fear of the death penalty will stop people from killing and committing crimes. Yet in truth it does not act as a deterrent at all. In fact the use of violence by society causes an increase of violence among its members. Fear does not work. Do we dare go so far as Jesus and say that it is useless?

Is there another path besides the way of fear? Is there another course of raising children besides the threat of punishment should they not behave? Is there another route toward creating a world of peace other than the escalation of weapons of mass destruction?

Christians are called to live another way. We are enjoined to live in trust, in faith. Today's gospel demonstrates how the way of trust leads to life. The woman is not healed by Jesus. She trusts in his ability and the healing power flows out of him and into her. Similarly Jesus exhorts the little girl's relatives to trust in him rather than to fear that it is too late. Then out of death Jesus calls her to life.

How do our own lives reveal our trust in God? Do we always presume that the worst will happen? Do we despair that things will never get better? Or do we exhibit trust in God? Do we seek to follow God's will for us in confidence that it will lead us to real happiness?

Paul suggests we are rich. How are we rich? We are rich through the favor shown us by Jesus Christ, who made himself poor so that we might share in the riches of his resurrection.

This abundance should persuade us to act generously toward others. We can afford to share our wealth so that all may experience equally the generosity of God's creation. We can afford to be rich in charity because we need not fear we will be left with nothing. So we can look upon others with the compassionate gaze of Jesus and make it possible for them also to share in the wealth of God's goodness.

CYCLE C

1 Kings 19:16, 19–21 Elisha rose and followed Elijah and became his servant.

Galatians 5:1, 13–18 My brothers, you were called to freedom.

Luke 9:51–62 Jesus resolutely set his face toward Jerusalem. I will follow you wherever you will go.

Today's gospel provides a number of the excuses we use not to follow Jesus' call. It is very easy for us to sit back and vegetate. But there is work to be done. Jesus has summoned each and every one of us to evangelize people.

There will always be business we think we should finish first. We usually do not need to seek for excuses as to why we cannot follow Jesus right away. One important reason we shy away from evangelization is that we believe we do not have enough talent or resources. Not so! Each of us has heard the scriptures for years. We pray. We share our faith with our children and with each other.

Jesus does not require us to take on the evangelization of the entire world. He is only asking us to take the next step. That we can certainly do. We do not need to know where we are going. Naturally we will resist such a step if we fathom from the outset that we are going to end up in Jerusalem and if we realize what that involves: suffering and death. But forget that for now. What is the next small step you as a Christian and we as a community can take to share the good news? Let us commit ourselves to that small measure and trust God to guide us from there.

Fourteenth Sunday of the Year

CYCLE A

Zechariah 9:9–10 See how humbly your king comes to you!

Romans 8:9, 11–13 If by the spirit you put an end to the misdeeds of the body, you will live.

Matthew 11:25–30 I am gentle and humble of heart.

The words of Jesus in the gospel today show wonderfully the treasure we have to share with the world: Jesus himself. He is our way to God. From him we receive all God's grace and gifts, especially the gift of the Holy Spirit. As Paul reminds us, that Spirit lives within us and raises us up from death to life.

This is the same gift that Jesus wishes us to share with all our brothers and sisters. We invite people to find Jesus so that they might find rest from their work and suffering. We desire that they might come to know the gentleness and mercy of God. This is the gift we have to share: no deep knowledge, only the love of God for us and the care God takes so that we might be safe.

CYCLE B

Ezekiel 2:2–5 The head of the house was annoyed; he knew there was a prophet in their midst.

2 Corinthians 12:7–10 I will glory in my infirmities so that the power of Christ may dwell in me.

Mark 6:1–6 A prophet is despised only in his own country.

Both the second reading and the gospel speak of humility. In the gospel, Jesus cannot perform miracles with those who know him. Paul speaks of the thorn in the flesh that he has asked to be removed. We are not beyond our faults and weaknesses as evangelists. God works through our blindness as well as our sight. Our failings are part of the gospel message.

If God can work through Paul and the saints with all their shortcomings (and each saint had many), God can work through you. Truly, precisely through our weakness God gains entrance into our lives. In powerlessness God's power reaches perfection. If we operate from our strength, we are not really preaching the gospel. In order to proclaim the good news we must begin from our lack and our helplessness. Evangelization is not interested in success. It does not matter if people listen to our message. Our duty is simply to proclaim and to live the good news. People will listen if God gives them the grace to hear. Ezekiel in the first reading receives this lesson. The people refuse to listen to him. However, his job is only to be true to the Word of God. The same task is ours.

CYCLE C

Isaiah 66:10–14 I will send toward Jerusalem peace like a river.

Galatians 6:14–18 The marks I carry on my body are those of Jesus Christ.

Luke 10:1–12,17–20 Your peace will rest upon him.

In today's sending forth of the seventy–two, Jesus provides down-to-earth, practical instructions. Naturally, many of these directions do not apply to our situation or our call to evangelize. But some do.

First of all, he sends them off two by two. A Christian is not a loner. We are before all else a community, a fellowship. Jesus is with us when two or three of us gather together. It is much easier to minister with others than alone.

Jesus further encourages us to pray as we minister. Our evangelization should arise out of, invite others into, and culminate in prayer. Our wonderful relationship to God in Jesus through the cross is indeed our good news.

He also cautions us to be on guard. We carry a message uncongenial to the world. We do not bring good news of how to become successful or powerful. We bring news of how to be reconciled in God and with one another. We might be seduced into carrying a message that is not the good news. We may be tempted to say what people want to hear. But that is not our task. Our task, as Paul reminds us, is to boast of nothing more than the cross: the death and resurrection of Jesus. We cannot afford to get sidetracked into politics or other questions. Let us keep our eyes firmly on our task.

Fifteenth Sunday of the Year

CYCLE A

Isaiah 55:10–11 The rain makes the earth fruitful.

Romans 8:18–23 All creation is waiting for God to reveal his children.

Matthew 13:1–23 A sower went out to sow.

The parable of the sower reveals a great deal about our mission to evangelize. To evangelize means to announce the good news of God's kingdom, which we have heard from and experienced in Jesus and his community. Imagine the seed of the parable as the Word of God or the gospel. Pretend you are the farmer sowing the seed. Scatter the seed to the wind: some falls on the rocks, some is eaten by the birds, some choked by weeds, but in spite of this there is a bountiful harvest.

Let us be prodigal when it comes to proclaiming the good news and sharing what Jesus means to us. Evangelization is not just done through carefully planned programs. It should be a risk-taking operation—scatter the seed everywhere. Sure, much of the time nothing will come up. But let us trust in God that the final harvest will be bountiful.

Also, as Isaiah points out, the Word of God with which we are entrusted is not inert or dead, but alive. It goes forth from God filled with the power to give life. And that Word returns to God bearing the new life that it has found. As participants in the ministry of this Word, we too share in the new life that it brings back to God. New people enrich our lives and our church. The Word produces life as the water brings life to the land. Here is an image of abundance and creation; it is a privilege to be part of Jesus' mission and to experience such glorious fullness and prosperity.

CYCLE B

Amos 7:12–15 Go, prophesy to my people.

Ephesians 1:3–14 Before the world was made, he chose us in Christ.

Mark 6:7–13 He called the Twelve, and began to send them out.

The gospel presents the poverty that the evangelist should embrace. Jesus sends out the disciples with nothing: just a walking stick. They must rely upon whatever happens in a particular situation. Stay in the house where you first arrive in the town. If they do not receive you, shake the dust from your sandals and move on. The work of evangelization is not about results or success. It consists in being faithful to the mission received from God. We succeed if we abide by our vocation to bring the good news to others. We are not judged by whether the others are able to hear and accept the good news.

While this teaching deters us from clinging to success or failure, it does not absolve us from presenting the good news to the best of our ability. We strive to announce the good news in a form that enables others to recognize in our evangelization the God whom we represent. Whether they come to know this God and believe in Him is not our concern. We sow the seeds. Others are responsible for the harvest.

CYCLE C

Deuteronomy 30:10–14 Let the instruction of the Lord God be near you.

Colossians 1:15–20 In him were created all things.

Luke 10:25–37 Who is my neighbor?

The first reading and the gospel speak of the Law. Jesus sums up the Law as love of God and love of neighbor. In a way a key means of evangelizing is simply to live up to what we believe. How can we show our love of God throughout our life? How does our community proclaim its love of God?

Earlier Christians proclaimed the love of God partly through their celebrations of feast days and festivals. It is difficult in the rush of life to stop and simply enjoy creation, and praise God for such a gift. But we might find ways in which our community could proclaim God's goodness through a celebration. If we could lead people toward play and enjoyment in the Lord, we would provide a crucial service for our overly busy world.

The second way we evangelize is to love our neighbor. Jesus shows by the parable of the Good Samaritan that there are no boundaries to who our neighbor is. The one next to us, whoever that may be, is our neighbor. We are called to love him or her as we love ourselves. Doing this is proclaiming, better still living, the good news.

Who are our neighbors in our parish? What people are living within our parish boundaries? How are we being neighbors to them? We might consider first our brothers and sisters, other Christians. Can we join with them in outreach to our neighbors? Then we should consider those neighbors who have no power and influence. What can we do to act as Good Samaritan to them?

Sixteenth Sunday of the Year

CYCLE A

Wisdom 12:13, 16–19 In the place of sin, you give repentance.

Romans 8:26–27 The Spirit himself pleads for us in a way that could never be put into words.

Matthew 13:24–43 Let them grow together until the harvest.

The gospel today continues the parables of the kingdom. The first parable, the weeds among the wheat, offers a glimpse into our ministry of evangelization. The seed has been sown. We have spoken the good news of Jesus to people and groups in our community. Once we have done our job let us not second-guess ourselves; do not worry about what could happen.

The parable speaks of opposition in the world. The good news we have to offer is not going to be accepted or understood by everyone. That is not our concern. Of course we will want to ask ourselves if we are indeed sharing the gospel as best we can. But once we have shared the word, grant God the time to allow that seed to come to fruition. After all, the seed and the succeeding wheat are both the Lord's; we are but the laborers.

The parable of the leaven shows that the kingdom of God is hidden at the center of all life. It gives life its lift, its flavor. But it is hidden. You cannot taste the leaven in the bread. Yet when it is absent we realize it immediately.

When we share the gospel with others, we do not partake of something apart from real life; we share the essence that gives life its zest. How do we recognize that essence, that leaven, in our own lives and community? How can we assist our neighbors in recognizing and coming to give thanks for that same leaven in their own lives?

CYCLE B

Jeremiah 23:1–6 The remnant of the flock I will gather to me, and bring them back to their pastures.

Ephesians 2:13–18 Christ is the peace between us.

Mark 6:30–34 They were as sheep without a shepherd.

Paul, in the second reading, speaks of Jesus' work as reconciliation. He broke down the barriers of hostility that divided us from each other. Once we were able to appreciate one another, we entered into a time of peace with one another as well as with God. This good news of peace is not restricted to an announcement to the world. God also calls for our participation in this peace. For it will refresh and strengthen us for our mission. It will ground us more deeply in Christ as it advances peace among different people.

Today's gospel reminds us of an important structure of the ministry of evangelization and indeed of all ministry. Furthermore, it is a component that we Americans are likely to neglect. Yet it is precisely this element that enables us to experience the peace of Christ in our life and our community. When the disciples come from their mission, Jesus draws them apart to rest.

Rest and withdrawal are an essential part of all ministry. Without it our ministry will dry up, and we will be unable to introduce people to the kingdom of God because we have ceased to experience it in our own life. We need to draw apart to rest, to pray, to share our experiences with one another: our successes, our failures.

Yes, our mission is huge. Many people are waiting to hear the good news and to feel Jesus' healing touch. It was the same in Jesus' day. The gospel speaks of such great numbers crowding around that it was impossible to so much as eat. However, this condition does not mean that we can afford to overlook times of rest, of retreat. Rest is as much a participation in the kingdom as is work.

CYCLE C

Genesis 18:1–10 Lord, do not bypass your servant.

Colossians 1:24–28 The mystery hidden for centuries has now been revealed to his saints.

Luke 10:38–42 Jesus speaks with Martha and Mary.

The first reading and today's gospel speak of hospitality, one of the key means of evangelization. We make people feel welcome, comfortable, and valued. Abraham receives the three visitors and makes them the center of his concern. Are you aware when someone new is at church? Surely you notice somebody whom you have not seen before. Perhaps you don't know if they are newcomers. What's the difference? If they are already parishioners you have gotten to know someone new. If they are visitors you have helped to make them feel at home.

This is such an ordinary task, but the size of our communities frightens us. Yet we are a family of brothers and sisters. It is important for us to get to know one another. And let us welcome those whom we discover are here for the first time. There is a grace in this as well. Because of his hospitality, Abraham and Sarah are rewarded with a child. Being hospitable invites new life to come into a family, a community, a church.

Seventeenth Sunday of the Year

CYCLE A

1 Kings 3:5, 7–12 He sought to give you wisdom.

Romans 8:28–30 He predestined us to become true images of his Son.

Matthew 13:44–52 He sells everything he owns, and buys the field.

Consider the first line in the second reading: We know that in everything God works for good with those who love God, who are called according to the divine purpose. This beautifully describes our mission as Christians. We have been asked to work for good along with God. God grants us the word of forgiveness, which God has spoken to all people. God entrusts us with the gift of healing which Jesus brings. We have been made aware of God and of God's love for us. We grasp God's plan for the world—God has reconciled us in Christ.

Knowing this, we live our lives in such a way that God's intention is furthered by us individually and communally. How is our community implementing the plan of God? How are we making it concrete in our public lives? In our families?

The dragnet is a wonderful image for evangelization. We proclaim the good news, and all sorts of wonderful people are attracted. Every kind of person on the face of the Earth is drawn in when they hear the good news. And we are the fishermen pulling these nets ashore: we extend our welcome to the people lured by seeing Jesus in us. They are different from us; they add to the awesome variety of God's kingdom, which is more like a grab bag than a matched set.

CYCLE B

2 Kings 4:42–44 They will eat and have some left over.

Ephesians 4:1–6 There is one body, one Lord, one faith, one baptism.

John 6:1–15 He distributed to those who were seated as much as they wanted.

The feeding of the people illustrates one of the key themes of the good news: abundance. As human beings we share the disciples' attitude; we do not believe we have enough. What we consider scarce changes according to the situation: bread, time, talent, patience, knowledge.

Yet a key sign of God's kingdom is abundance. The feeding stories always feature lots of leftovers. No one goes away hungry. Such abundance appears in other places: in Jesus' healings, in the lives of the early Christians when they shared their possessions and lived in common.

To be true evangelizers, we too must make present to people God's abundance. In our parish functions, is there always more than needed? Is there always room and welcome for one more? Is there a reliance upon God's generosity? What are some ways people might see and experience the abundance and generosity of God in our community?

In the second reading, Paul furnishes another central theme of evangelization: the unity of all in Christ. We witness to a God who gathers what is divided and brings all into one community, one spirit. All the barriers separating people are dissolved, and we discover our communion with all peoples and world cultures.

In order for us to witness to this unity, we ourselves need to be united. And we can only realize this if we act with the qualities Paul mentions at the beginning of the reading: humility, meekness, and patience.

It is not easy to live as one. We appreciate this from the difficulty we experience in marriage: in spite of the fact that we love our spouse and our children, it is not easy for us to be united. We have different notions and visions. For unity to be achieved, we must be willing to listen and then to compromise. But the experience of that unity is so wonderful that in retrospect the things sacrificed seem of little value.

CYCLE C

Genesis 18:20–32 Lord, do not be angry if I speak.

Colossians 2:12–14 He has made you alive with Christ, for he has forgiven all our sins.

Luke 11:1–13 Ask, and it will be given to you.

Paul shocks us with the enormous scope of the good news. While we were still dead, still in sin, God gave us new life in the friendship of Jesus and pardoned our sins. It is very easy to twist the good news into the not so good news. We are tempted to distort the gospel to make it say that only if you turn from your sin will God pardon you. But this is not really good news. How is this different from the way the world runs?

No, while we were still in sin, God reached out to us in Jesus and died for us, unworthy as we were and are. God has already reconciled the world in Jesus' cross. And that means God has already reconciled all sinners past, present, and future. The gospel proclaims that this reconciliation has happened. Now in the light of what God has done, what is your response? God has already buried your sins in the grave with Christ. Will you not come and be part of the victory feast thrown in your honor?

Eighteenth Sunday of the Year

CYCLE A

Isaiah 55:1–3 Hasten and eat.

Romans 8:35,37–39 No creature can separate us from the love of God, which is in Christ.

Matthew 14:13–21 They all ate and were satisfied.

The first and third readings reveal a major theme of the good news: God's overwhelming abundance and generosity. Isaiah invites all to come to the banquet and astonishes us by adding that this banquet is free and open to all who thirst and are hungry, whether they have money or not. In our culture, money is often the only thing that counts. If you have money you are "in" and part of the society; if you do not, you are "out." It does not matter how you got your money: whether you earned, inherited, or embezzled it (as long as you are not caught), the money itself is your admission card to the banquet.

However, God does not traffic in currency but rather in need. The price of admission is simple want: thirst and hunger.

The gospel builds upon Isaiah. Jesus is teaching the crowd, but the disciples are worried that people will become hungry and unruly. They want Jesus to disperse the people before they realize their hunger. However Jesus responds as God does in Isaiah. Indeed he feeds the hungry before they are conscious of being hungry. Such abundance and generosity are signs of God and God's kingdom.

As Jesus' followers we too are signs of God's abundance and generosity. How do we as individuals and as our church community show forth that abundance? What do we do to feed the hungry? To give drink to the thirsty? When our parish has an event, is it a sign of God's abundance and generosity? Is there always plenty for all? Are we welcoming of any strangers who might wander in?

CYCLE B

Exodus 16:2–4,12–15 I will rain bread from heaven upon you.

Ephesians 4:17, 20–24 Put on the new person that has been created in God's image.

John 6:24–35 Whoever comes to me will never be hungry; whoever believes in me will never thirst.

Today's first reading and gospel focus upon the Eucharist, the center of our life as Catholic Christians. The Eucharist is the sign of God's love for us and God's abiding presence in our midst. However, as the gospel indicates, signs can be mistaken or poorly perceived. We must attempt to verbalize, however inadequately, what the Eucharist signifies. Non-Catholics have many misperceptions of the Eucharist's meaning. While the sign of Eucharist may be drawing them toward the faith, they still must come to an understanding of what we believe concerning the central action of our faith. It may appear to some as magical. But it is not magic. On the other hand, it may appear to be simply a group celebration, and we certainly consider the Eucharist far more than that.

We do not, however, need to trot out all the old theological arguments about the Eucharist. The first reading describes how the miraculous manna fed the Israelites as they wandered around the wilderness for forty years. The Eucharist is our daily bread as well. But it is not simply physical food—it feeds our spirits. And just how does it do this? What do we experience when we attend the Eucharist? How are we nourished? How are we given food for spiritual growth?

How does our own community regard the Eucharist? What do we have to say about it? Remember we are a community of Christians—we are not solitary individuals! Furthermore, our community of faith stretches back through history as well as across today's geography. What did our ancestors say about the Eucharist that is still nourishing for us? Above all, we can share our experiences of the Eucharist with one another. Such sharing will not only equip us with words to break open the Eucharist for others, but it will deepen our own appreciation and understanding of this great mystery celebrated daily in our midst.

CYCLE C

Ecclesiastes 1:2;2:21–23 What do all his labors profit a man?

Colossians 3:21–5,9–11 Seek the things that are above where Christ is.

Luke 12:13–21 Why are you preparing these things?

We are people of Spirit. For us the material world is not our final concern or goal. We do not spurn it; we enjoy it. But we know it is not permanent; it is not lasting. To try to hold on to possessions, prestige, wealth, and health is ultimately foolish, as the preacher reminds us in the first reading.

Jesus provides an even stronger example in the parable. The good capitalist of the parable, concerned about shoring up and insuring his security, misses out on the true richness of life. It is hard to be a Christian in a materialistic culture. It is hard to resist the lure of advertising that dangles each new product before us as the answer to our dreams.

Many people today are beginning to see the shallow satisfactions of materialism. They are searching for something more. They are in search of the spiritual. And we have what they are looking for. As Paul tells us, we have set our hearts on things above rather than on things of earth. How might we be a witness to our neighbors of this higher way? How do we aid them in their struggle for fulfillment?

We do not need to condemn our culture. It has provided for the first time in history the possibility of a high standard of living for the greatest number. But while it provides us with many benefits and luxuries, it cannot in itself satisfy our deepest longings—for community, for relationships, for transcendence of our small selves. Here Christians can bear witness. Where do we place our values and trust? How do we occupy our time? What is the place of material goods in our homes? Our fellow Americans are looking for the Spirit. How might we live so that they recognize what they seek in Jesus Christ?

Nineteenth Sunday of the Year

CYCLE A

1 Kings 19:9, 11–13 Go out and stand on the mountain before the Lord God.

Romans 9:1–5 I would willingly be condemned if it would help my brother or sister.

Matthew 14:22–33 Command me to come to you over the waters.

Some of us may be tempted to read the gospel today as a judgment against Peter because of his impetuous desire to walk on water. We see Jesus and Christianity as a way of caution and propriety. How dare Peter want to walk on water? Such an action is for Jesus alone. I am humble; I would never make such a request. Look what happens to Peter! He sinks and needs to be rescued. However, the story does not rebuke Peter's impulsiveness so much as his lack of trust. Trust is at the heart of our faith. Indeed *trust* is a much better synonym for "faith" than the usual *belief*.

As people of faith we trust in God. We trust God to support us and carry us through, even when, like Peter, we make fools of ourselves and fail. In what do we trust? Well, of course, in God we trust. But how does this work itself out in our lives? How do we find God's presence in our daily life?

The story of Elijah provides wisdom for seeking God. God is not to be found in the hurricanes, earthquakes, or fires, although God is certainly there too. But God comes in the still small voice, the hint half-heard. Do we dare to trust that voice and follow it? If we do we make our faith active, when people witness our trust of God's presence and guidance they will be drawn to us. We are certainly not people who do not make mistakes. Peter seems to make a mistake every time he opens his mouth. But his trust in Jesus is his salvation—weak though it may be in this story. Our trust in the voice of God proclaims who we are.

CYCLE B

1 Kings 19:4–8 Strengthened by the food, he walked to the mountain of the Lord.

Ephesians 4:30–5:2 Walk in love, just as Christ.

John 6:41–51 I am the living bread that came down from heaven.

The beginning of today's gospel reiterates a necessary point relevant to our efforts at evangelization. We do not bring people to Christ. God draws the person. Meditating upon this insight should both make us humble and lift a great weight from our shoulders. Evangelization, like all ministry, is not a doing but really a cooperating and an enabling. We cooperate with God in helping a person come to know Jesus. And, as we see from today's gospel, there are people who will not be able to see Jesus as we do. They will reject our message, and they will ostensibly reject him as well. If we have done our part and tried our best to tell of Jesus and his good news, we need have no sense of failure. The dynamic of a person's coming to know and accept God is a mystery. We cannot compel it to happen or force it. We can only make ourselves available to aid God in this wonderful encounter.

CYCLE C

Wisdom 18:6–9 Just as you struck our enemies, you make us glorious by calling us to you.

Hebrews 11:1–2, 8–19 We will look for the city designed and built by God.

Luke 12:32–48 See that you are prepared.

Two themes from today's readings flesh out the task of evangelization: faith and readiness. The second reading lauds the faith of Abraham and Sarah. They trusted in the promises of God. And they dared to live their lives supported by faith in God. The author mentions that they did not receive what had been promised before they died, yet they had trust nonetheless. We are asked to live in the same faith. We believe in Jesus' power over sickness and death; we trust that good ultimately will triumph over evil. So we dare to live our lives with this confidence. Such faith does not banish sickness, death, or evil. They may seem all too powerful in our life or world, yet in faith we do not succumb and abandon hope. We keep faith not only to sustain our own life and to support our fellow believers, but we do so to witness to others what we believe. When Christians enter the fight against poverty or AIDS or other struggles that seem impossible to win, we do so because we have faith that God is with us, and whether we win or not God's will shall eventually prevail.

Jesus calls us to be watchful. Vigilance plays a key role in our ministry of evangelization. Not every moment is the same. We must discern the opportune occasion in which to share the good news. Some Christians attempt to evangelize in practically every situation. Perhaps they have tried to evangelize us. They think all you have to do is keep on plugging away. But true mission cannot be so mindless. There is a time and a place for everything, including proclaiming God's Word. Be watchful for that time! Then let us be wise in just how we share the gospel, so that it becomes not an advertisement but an invitation. To do this demands prayer and vigilance on our part.

Twentieth Sunday of the Year

CYCLE A

Isaiah 56:1, 6–7 My children who come to me I will lead to my holy mountain.

Romans 11:13–15, 29–32 The gifts and call of God are irrevocable.

Matthew 15:21–28 Woman, your faith is great.

The second and third readings today speak of the boundaries of God's mercy. Many people want to put up limits to God's benevolence. Certainly for nearly two thousand years Christians were willing to consign Israel to God's wrath because she rejected Christ. Yet as Paul grapples with the question, he stumbles upon the mystery of God's mercy. God has consigned everyone to disobedience, in order to have mercy upon all. There are really no boundaries to God's compassion. Israel may have rejected Jesus, but that rejection is mysteriously a part of God's design so that God might show mercy to all.

Jesus himself seems to have felt that there were limits to God's mercy, that is until he met this wonderful Canaanite woman. She pushes his limits and opens him up to the realization that his ministry may reach beyond the tribes of Israel. She is doubly marginal: neither a Jew nor a man. Yet she convinces Jesus to act for her and her daughter. When we think of the good news we have been given to proclaim, we must also consider the people who might hear our good news. We are sent not only to the acceptable people, whoever they might be in our minds, but to all people. For in the mystery of the kingdom, God has determined that mercy shall be poured out upon all—not just a chosen few. Do we speak and live the good news in a way that all people have a chance to hear the invitation? Or do we speak only to those we find acceptable?

CYCLE B

Proverbs 9:1–6 Come and eat my bread, drink the wine I have prepared.

Ephesians 5:15–20 Be watchful that you may know the will of God.

John 6:51–58 My flesh is real food and my blood is real drink.

Today's gospel goes to the heart of Catholic understanding of the Eucharist; it is the Bread of Life. By joining with others who celebrate this mystery we already have a glimpse of eternal life. At this very moment we are lifted up from death and feel the power of the resurrection within us. We experience this because the bread we eat is the very body and blood of Jesus Christ. John's language is unquestionably strong: he talks about gnashing on the flesh of Christ and drinking his blood.

Our strong belief in the significance of the Eucharist gives it such a central location in Catholic life. It has given rise to devotions like the Benediction and Perpetual Adoration. It leads us to genuflect whenever we come into the presence of the Holy Bread. The reservation of that bread sanctifies the space of our churches.

The presence of God made sacramental in the eucharistic bread brings people to our church in search of the holy. In our churches they sense the presence of the divine. In our evangelization we need to assure people that, yes, this is what we believe. They are often searching for this very pledge of God's presence. Being human beings and having bodies, we long for a bodily manifestation of God. We Catholics have that guarantee in the Eucharistic bread and wine.

CYCLE C

Jeremiah 38:4–6, 8–10 You bore me to be a man of strife for the whole world.

Hebrews 12:1–4 Let us bear patiently the struggle placed upon us.

Luke 12:49–53 I have come not to give peace, but discord.

The first two readings today show us another side of evangelization: the role of the martyr. A martyr is a witness to God's word. That witness is often met by the world's hostility and rejection. Jeremiah is following his commission from God to speak truth to Israel. But it is a word Israel does not want to hear; and Jeremiah is cast into the cistern. Jesus also suffers such rejection. Although we have good news, gospel, to announce, such good news is not always easy or nice to hear. We know this from our own lives: not only in the past but again and again the gospel challenges us to abandon sinful ways and embrace the way of life. Proclaiming the good news often reveals the tragedy of our situation, and we do not like having our misery so exposed.

We too are called to be witnesses, and we must sometimes witness to unpopular causes. The gospel does not always go down like honey. Sometimes it tastes of gall. We live in a society that does not value life, yet we are called to prize life supremely and to take stands against death, whether abortion, capital punishment, euthanasia, or economic oppression. We may be hated or ridiculed for espousing such causes.

We need to find the appropriate ways so that our message of life can be heard. It is not enough to shout out our cause obnoxiously. It is not permitted us to use the tactics of violence and threat in the cause of life. But let us be on fire, like Jesus, to endure the cross for the joy set before us.

Twenty-First Sunday of the Year

CYCLE A

Isaiah 22:15,19–21 I place the key of the house of David upon his shoulder.

Romans 11:33–36 From him, through him, and in him are all things.

Matthew 16:13–20 You are Peter, to you I will give the keys of the kingdom of heaven.

Who do you say that I am? Evangelization tries to answer this question. Who is Jesus for us? It will not do us any good merely to echo Peter's response: You are the Christ. Everyone knows this today, but for most people "the Christ" is at best the last name of Jesus or at worst an empty phrase. We must find our own answer for ourselves and for our age. What does Jesus mean to you? Who is he for you? Who is he for our community?

An answer to this question is not the end of evangelization but merely an invitation. Words and names can only point to the reality of God. God is beyond all words and concepts. We wish to help people enter into the wonder of Saint Paul in the second reading. Evangelization should help people to experience for themselves the glory of God. Then they in turn can answer for themselves, "Who do you say that I am?"

CYCLE B

Josiah 24:1–2, 15–17, 18 We will serve the Lord God, because the Lord is our God.

Ephesians 5:21–32 This is the great mystery. It applies to Christ and the Church.

John 6:60–69 Lord, to whom shall we go? You have the words of eternal life.

The teaching that the Eucharist is the flesh and blood of Christ is difficult to believe (or swallow, if you will). It commands us to go beyond our senses and against common sense. It has never been easy: in today's gospel many disciples leave Jesus after this discourse. Notice that these are disciples, not just people in the crowd. These people have been following him, listening to him teach, and seeing him work signs. Yet they cannot stomach this teaching.

The gospel demands a decision from us. Are you with Jesus or not? To say "Yes" is not easy. We may not be able to justify our decision. Like Peter we may have nowhere else to go or no one else to follow.

Doubt is difficult to accept. Often Christians hope it will go away. But we are afraid to talk about it. What if it reveals that I do not really have faith? What if my doubt makes me seem deficient in others' eyes? Everyone doubts.

Inquirers need to know that Christians also have doubt—about God, about Christ, about the Eucharist.

But more than this, they and we need to know how we live with and sometimes overcome our doubts and disbelief. We are obliged to share with others and with each other the true ups and downs of our faith life, even if it means sighing with Peter: we don't know where else to go.

CYCLE C

Isaiah 66:18–21 They will gather all of your brothers and sisters from all nations.

Hebrews 12:5–7,11–13 The Lord disciplines those he loves.

Luke 13:22–30 People from the east and from the west will come to take their place in the kingdom of God.

The second reading and gospel may be read as a call to discipline, not exactly a contemporary value. We want everything now and without effort. Yet discipline is necessary for growth. Without discipline the artist does not develop craft. Without discipline we do not mature spiritually. We cannot acquire wisdom by reading a book or listening to a homily. Unless we do the hard work of praying and being shaped, we are not converted.

Yet we want to rescue the notion of discipline from the obsolete and abusive childrearing metaphor used by the author of Hebrews. We now know that "spare the rod and spoil the child" will not help a child grow. But what of the hardships that come into our own life? Do we see them as a possibility for discipline and for our growth? Or do we try to avoid them, narcotize ourselves against them, pray that they will go away? We are being molded by God. Everything that happens to us is God's will to aid our transformation. We are engaged in a dangerous work, and Jesus' admonitions address not outsiders but his own people—ourselves. We have been chosen for an awesome task. More will be expected of us because more has been given us, both as Christians and as Americans. If we do not take this commission seriously, if we do not accept discipline and allow ourselves to be converted so that we shine with the gospel, we risk being left behind while others to whom this wondrous opportunity has not been given enter the kingdom before us.

Twenty-Second Sunday of the Year

CYCLE A

Jeremiah 20:7–9 The word of the Lord has meant derision for me.

Romans 12:1–3 May you present your bodies as a living sacrifice.

Matthew 16:21–27 If anyone wishes to come after me, let them deny themselves.

Perhaps we have the impression that evangelization is something we do from strength, if we have the time and resources. But our life is not always lived from strength—we have times of failure, of sickness, of rejection. The gospel speaks to those times just as much if not more so than to seasons of plenty and happiness. Paul tells us to make our bodies a sacrifice to God. Jeremiah laments his miserable lot as a prophet: unheard and rejected by the people. Jesus looks forward to his own rejection and death.

Peter may speak for many of us who would prefer to look only at the good side of things. Yet God speaks to our misery as well. When we are sick, we can be just as much a sign of the good news as when we are well. Truly the Sacrament of the Sick speaks of the patient as a sign of

Christ suffering. It all rests upon how we see our illness. Do we see it as the world does—useless and meaningless—or do we see it as part of turning ourselves over to God and God's will for us? If we see it as the latter, we allow our minds to be converted.

CYCLE B

Deuteronomy 4:1–2,6–8 You may add nothing to the word which I speak to you—keep the commands of the Lord.

James 1:17–18, 21–22, 27 Be doers of the word.

Mark 7:1–8, 14–15, 21–23 You forget the commandments of God and hold on to human traditions.

All three readings underline the necessity to put into practice what we claim to believe. No more powerful witness to the gospel exists than the actions of a Christian which evince the spirit of Christ. A community filled with compassion and continually looking after the outcast and the poor (James's widows and orphans) is engaging in evangelization more effectively than one that merely proclaims the words, even if employing the vast resources of modern media.

Let us put aside words today, although words are certainly necessary. How would people know about Jesus through our actions alone? How do our church's activities in our community exemplify the good news? How does what we do in our family, in our work, in our community proclaim the gospel we have received from Jesus?

CYCLE C

Sirach 3:17–18, 20, 28–29 Humble yourself and you will find favor with the Lord.

Hebrews 12:18–19. 22–24 You have come to Mount Zion and to the city of the living God.

Luke 14:1, 7–14 Whoever exalts self shall be humbled and whoever humbles self shall be exalted.

Sirach and the gospel today speak of humility. This is not a currently popular virtue. We wish our good actions to be known and recognized. Yet humility is recommended; our deeds might be hidden, unperceived. Yet they are deeds nonetheless. If we apply this notion to evangelization, we see that in order for us to be sowers of the word it is not necessary that we be recognized and honored. What we do, we do not for our own sakes but for the sake of others—all of whom are beloved by God. Evangelization is not something the church does in order to gain new members, to become the biggest, to get the world to see that we are the center of it all. Evangelization is something we do because God has instructed us to reach out to others with our gifts and values without expecting any return, simply because we are imitating God's own infinite generosity and humility.

Twenty-Third Sunday of the Year

CYCLE A

Ezekiel 33:7–9 If you have not warned the wicked one, then I will hold you responsible for their death.

Romans 13:8–10 Love is the fulfillment of the law.

Matthew 18:15–20 If they listen to you, you have won back your brother or sister.

We may be tempted to think of evangelization as a marketing ploy for God. We are out to convert the entire world. We want to convince everyone to join the church.

But the second reading and the gospel speak of our lives in an ordinary and humble way. Paul asks us to love our neighbor—if we can do that we are fulfilling the entire law.

It is such a simple command, yet how hard to live! It is easier to dream up and execute some great five-year plan that would draw the world to us. Simply loving our neighbor may appear too ordinary. But to do so would radically change our lives and our world.

Jesus does not speak of a community that is worldwide but of two or three who gather in his name and follow his way. There he is present. To be evangelizers does not require more than living the gospel—loving our neighbor, following Jesus' way of forgiveness and healing. More than any program, such behavior reveals the mystery of God in our community and world.

CYCLE B

Isaiah 35:4–7 Then the ears of the deaf shall be opened and the tongues of the dumb speak.

James 2:1–5 Has not God chosen the poor of the world to inherit the kingdom?

Mark 7:31–37 He has made the deaf hear and the dumb speak.

The readings from Isaiah and Mark both speak of openings: opening the ears of the deaf, the eyes of the blind, the waters in the desert. The image of opening serves as a metaphor for the good news. When we really hear the gospel our world opens up: we see and hear things as though for the first time. There is a sense of excitement. In the gospel Jesus charges the dumb man whom he heals to tell no one of the event. But how could he keep such news secret? Instead he goes out to tell everybody what happened to him.

As evangelists, we are also given good news to tell. Yet unlike the man cured in today's gospel, we are shy of telling what we have experienced. What has the gospel opened in our lives and in our community?

How have our eyes been opened to a different vision of people so that, as James writes, we do not treat people according to their social status but as beloved of God? How does our parish community help us mature in this vision of God's love for all? How does our parish exhibit to the community outside this wonderful revelation?

What are the openings in our life? What examples do we have of people being opened to the gospel? What of the stories our catechumens tell? How does our parish community through our acceptance of evangelization provide an opening into the larger community? What might such openings look like?

CYCLE C

Wisdom 9:13–18 Who can comprehend the will of God?

Philemon 1:9–10, 12–17 Receive him, not as a slave anymore, but as a very dear brother.

Luke 14:25–33 Whoever who does not renounce their possessions cannot be my disciple.

In today's gospel, Jesus emphasizes through powerful images what must ground our whole life—the love of God. All our actions and words will fail unless they are established in God's love. If anything of ourselves and our self-love—whether for ego or church—is present in our preaching and showing forth of the word, our work will be useless and will not truly be God's work.

When Jesus speaks here of father, mother, and family, he is not saying that the family is not good or important. Indeed this is often where we first learn of and experience the love of God. But this disturbing image underlines the necessity of a sure foundation—commitment to and love of God as we find God in Jesus: his life and his words. Such love must stand behind all our efforts at evangelization.

We are not concerned to increase our church membership, to get people to realize that Catholics are the best Christians, or to win over the world to the one true faith. We are opening ourselves to others in love because we have first been embraced by Jesus. What we have received we cannot help but share. We must trust in this love. We cannot use it to coerce or manipulate without seriously distorting it into something that is not gospel. We can only live by it and trust in Jesus.

Twenty-Fourth Sunday of the Year

CYCLE A

Sirach 27:30–28:7 Forgive your neighbor's faults, and when you pray, your sins will be forgiven.

Romans 14:7–9 Whether alive or dead, we belong to the Lord.

Matthew 18:21–35 I tell you to forgive not seven times but seventy times seven.

Paul points out that our lives are not our own. We have turned them over to God. Or rather we have returned them to God, whose creation they are in the first place. We are not to live to ourselves but to the Lord. And we die to the Lord as well. If we try to live more and more in conformity with the Lord, it will involve a great deal of dying.

To live according to the gospel often resembles death.

Consider how difficult it is to forgive someone. All sorts of excuses tempt us. If I forgive them, they will assume it is an invitation to take advantage of me. If I forgive them, I appear weak. What about me and my feelings!

Such may be the servant's thoughts in today's gospel as he encounters his fellow servant and demands his ten cents back. He has forgotten how much he has been forgiven. Not one of us could survive without God's constant forgiveness. We are forgiven not just when we first wake up to Christ. We are constantly in need of reconciliation throughout our Christian journey, because we continually sin and fall short. God's forgiveness is guaranteed whenever we need it. But for the kingdom of God to come it is necessary that this forgiveness flow from us in turn. Think of all the people and groups who do not deserve forgiveness. We all have lists of such people. One of our missions of evangelization is indeed to forgive each of these people. Only by forgiveness that flows from us may they recognize the merciful grace that begins from God. We do not forgive because we are nice or good. We forgive because we have been forgiven and are commanded to forgive in turn.

CYCLE B

Isaiah 50:4–9 I gave my body to those who struck me.
James 2:14–18 Faith without good works is dead.
Mark 8:27–35 You are the Christ...the Son of Man, was destined to suffer much.

In the second reading, James provides an opportunity to speak of evangelization in terms of works. A popular idea of evangelization involves preaching or proselytizing, asking others about their faith. But faith without works is dead. Our works show forth our faith. Consider some of the works of our community or of the Christian Church. Missionaries have always brought literacy and medical aid along with the good news. By what missions does our community incarnate Christ's charity? How do these works point to the faith that undergirds them?

The gospel provides another entry into evangelization in the image of the Christian taking up the cross to deny self. Isaiah expands upon this image. Here the good person is a sign and imitation of the one we follow. The cross is at the very center of our faith. We believe for every death there is hope of resurrection. So the cross is the focal point of our evangelization as well. We have nothing else to present to the world but Jesus' cross: our cross. While our world shrinks from death and tries to deny it, Christians embrace it because we trust we will be raised up. How do we present the cross in our lives?

In our world, the cross is a great sign. These signs, like advertising logos, may be vehicles of evangelization or simply decorations. Each Catholic church displays the cross prominently. Many are drawn to our churches for a place of quiet. While there they will see the cross. How do we help them begin to explore the depth of this sign in our lives? How do we help others as well as ourselves to recognize the deep mystery which the cross both reveals and hides?

Many Christians wear crosses. Are these simply ornaments or can they become vehicles of evangelization? If you wear a cross, are you prepared to witness to it? Are you ready to share its meaning for you with others?

CYCLE C

Exodus 32:7–11, 13–14 The Lord relented and did not send the evil he had threatened.

1 Timothy 1:12–17 Christ came to save sinners.

Luke 15:1–32 There will be joy in heaven over one sinner who does penance.

Jesus in the gospel spells out what our task, our outlook should be. We are not here to focus upon our present community. Yes, the church certainly exists to instruct, nourish, and reconcile its members. But this is only the foundation of church—the setting up of the structure. The church really exists to go out in search of what is lost and to bring that lost thing of wondrous value into the community rejoicing in the homecoming. A Christian can never write off those who are suffering, poor, drug addicted, criminal, or persecuted. These are God's special loved ones whom we are sent to bring into our family, to share God's hospitality and mercy.

We might define *evangelization* in terms of those who are lost and found. However if we attend closely, we are all of us in some way still lost and still constantly being found. We have truly not yet begun to understand and appreciate God's love and mercy. Yes, some people are worse off than us. But they cannot be said to be damned while we are saved. As Paul points out next week, God desires the salvation of the entire human race.

Sin may separate us from God, but sin has been reconciled in Jesus Christ. Now all that intervenes between us and God's mercy is ignorance, says Paul. We are not in a game of who is in and who is left out, but on a mission to enfold the entire human race into God's mercy. The greater the sin, the lostness, the lameness, the blindness, the deadness, the greater the forgiveness, the foundness, the healing, the raising to life. Rejoicing is the only appropriate response.

Today's gospel concludes with the story of the prodigal son, and here again we see the blurring of boundaries. The prodigal son sees himself as a sinner. The elder brother sees himself as righteous. But the father only sees two sons, one of whom was lost. All the father can do is throw the feast and rejoice. If the elder brother cannot overcome his sense of righteousness, he will go hungry and will miss a great celebration.

Twenty-Fifth Sunday of the Year

CYCLE A

Isaiah 55:6–9 My thoughts are not your thoughts.

Philippians 1:20–24, 27 For me to live is Christ.

Matthew 20:1–16 Why are you jealous because I am generous?

Today's first reading and gospel highlight the mystery and inscrutability of God. True, we know that God is love, is merciful, all-knowing, and all-powerful. But God is ultimately still unknown: a mystery. We cannot possibly comprehend God or God's ways. Really, we might trust as a sure sign we are in God's presence those occasions when we are dumbfounded, like the servants in the parable who expected a great increase in their wages based on what those hired last received.

All we know is that God loves us and has claimed us. That knowledge should enable us to let go of ourselves so that God's plan for us may unfold. Paul speaks of being indifferent whether he lives or dies. What a sign of trust in God! If we can emulate Paul, people may catch a glimpse of the God who has claimed us as God's own.

CYCLE B

Wisdom 2:17–20 Let us condemn him to a most shameful death.

James. 3:16–4:3 Justice is the harvest of peacemakers from seeds sown in a spirit of peace.

Mark 9:30–37 The Son of Man will be delivered into the hands of men....If anyone wishes to be first, he must make himself the servant of all

The righteous person appears in all three readings today: in Wisdom as a signal that provokes the unrighteous to attack; in James as a model for Christian existence—the person not ruled by passion; in Mark as the fulfillment of the righteous person in Wisdom who is killed but vindicated by God through resurrection. We evangelize primarily through who we are. We ourselves are called to be the good news to the world. If we imitate Jesus—the righteous one—and live not ruled by passion, but by love and compassion, we will attract people toward the truth. They will want to know what motivates us: Why do we act as we do? By asking this question they invite us to tell our story: how we have been touched and converted by the righteous one, Jesus.

Another approach centers on the last line of today's gospel: Whoever receives one such child in my name receives me. Teaching children the gospel is a dimension of evangelization. Children in Jesus' society were not valued for who they were but for who they might become. The disciples want to keep them away from Jesus. They thought the children would be a distraction from Jesus' true mission. However, Jesus demonstrates how all are valued and loved by God.

What does our parish do for children? How is the parish school involved in the mission of evangelization? Does the school provide an opportunity for all children to experience God's love? Are there programs for local children that illustrate for them and the community God's love and abundance? Catechesis of children is largely evangelization—we are introducing the children to God and allowing them to experience God's love.

CYCLE C

Amos 8:4–7 The Lord God spoke against those who buy the poor for money.

1 Timothy 2:1–8 Let prayers be offered to God for everyone, for God wishes that everyone be saved.

Luke 16:1–13 You cannot be slaves both of God and of money.

Evangelization must include a drive for social justice. For our God is a God of justice. And this justice must be that of God, and not that of human beings, particularly those who wield power. Justice pleads for those who are weak, poor, and voiceless. Those in power are not only capable of helping themselves, but, as Amos points out, are inevitably driven to help themselves at the expense of those in need. Certainly we cannot look at our current tax and welfare structure in the light of Amos's words without wincing. It is not that we are bad, but that we are human. These words apply to current conditions just as they did in Amos's time.

So our witnessing to the gospel means that, like Jesus, we first turn to the exiled, the weak, the poor, the powerless, those without a voice. To them is the word of comfort and hope first spoken. And it is not by words alone that we must speak; words are cheap. We speak the gospel by our actions. Do we as Christians stand up for the poor and hungry? Do we feed individuals as well as seek for structures of justice by which poverty can be eliminated?

But, like Amos, we must also address the gospel message to power. This task is not comfortable, especially if we ourselves share in this power, as do most American Catholics. We are tempted not to rock the boat, not to bite the hand that feeds us. Don't upset things if we are relatively well-off ourselves. Yet God and Jesus call us beyond self interest to speak and do the truth.

When we are in power, we tend to have a different view of justice than when we are powerless. So we can scoff at welfare mothers and deadbeat dads, drug addicts, AIDS sufferers; we can give up hope on criminals once they have transgressed three times. Yet Jesus turns the image of justice on its head. The servant acts unjustly in the sight of the world. The world expects that a servant will not cheat his master. But Jesus commends the unjust steward who is weak and who shrewdly does what is necessary to save his skin. Jesus asks us to be just as shrewd as we look at the world. Who is in need, and how can we enable those who have less to enter into their share of the inheritance God intends for all?

Twenty-Sixth Sunday of the Year

CYCLE A

Exodus 18:25–28 When the sinner decides to turn against their sinfulness, they deserve to live.

Philippians 2:1–11 In your minds be as Jesus Christ.

Matthew 21:28–32 He went out moved by regret. The tax

collectors and prostitutes will precede you into the kingdom of God.

The beautiful hymn Paul quotes in the second reading offers a great example of how to live the gospel and to proclaim it in our lives. Let us live for others. This is what Jesus did. Dietrich Bonhoeffer, a modern theologian, named him, "The man who lived for others." The way of Jesus is not a way that puts ourselves first, but rather looks to the needs of others. It is a way of self-forgetfulness. We are loved, of that Jesus assures us. Assured of that love, we can turn our attention elsewhere. As individuals and as community, we should be known for our regard for others. Are we seen as reaching out in help? Is our church recognized for its aid to the poor, its voice given to the voiceless, its concern for those otherwise forgotten? If not, we are like the son in the parable who says he will do what his father asks and then does not. Which son did the will of the father?

CYCLE B

Numbers 11:25–29 Are you jealous on my account? Who decrees that all people may prophesy?

James 5:1–6 Your wealth is rotting.

Mark 9:38–43, 45, 47–48 Anyone who is not against us is for us. If your hand should cause you to sin, cut it off.

One evangelization theme from today's readings lies in realizing that when we evangelize we are putting ourselves in the service of God's spirit. We may have evangelization plans and strategies, but ultimately God has the master plan, which is unlikely to be identical with our own. We are called to preach and proclaim the good news. This does not mean propagandizing for our own parish or even our own denomination. Evangelization is wider than any boundaries we might draw. God wishes all creation to hear the good news, and therefore God chooses many messengers and many messages to carry this word.

In Numbers, the people are upset with the two prophets who are not following the established order. Similarly, in the gospel the disciples encounter other people who are casting out demons in Jesus' name and want him to put a stop to it. In evangelization we will find others working together with us. Catholics encounter fundamentalist Christians in the witness against abortion. We sit side by side with Jews and Buddhists in the peace movement. We have found ourselves allied with Marxists in the struggle for justice.

Evangelization has ecumenical and even inter-religious dimensions. We are all called to bear good news. When we find ourselves with others who are not of our community, our church, or even our faith, we may recognize them as our sisters and brothers. We work for a common good. We are not in competition with one another; instead we might explore more deeply the unity we share already, and the unity God desires us to realize more fully.

The last section of the gospel offers another approach to evangelization. Living the gospel demands discipline, or to use the traditional word, ascesis. The gospel calls us to conversion and transformation. We do not have a message to preach; we have a message to live, which transforms us. Jesus' images are harsh and are not meant to be taken literally. But before we can adequately proclaim the gospel to others, we must first be evangelized ourselves. The gospel must first convert our parish. As we come to embody the good news in ourselves and our church, we, by that very making flesh of the gospel, become signs of God's love to our brothers and sisters.

CYCLE C

Amos 6:3, 4–7 You who give yourself to licentiousness and revelry will be exiled.

1 Timothy 6:11–16 Obey the commandments until the coming of the Lord.

Luke 16:19–31 During your life good things came your way just as bad things came the way of Lazarus. Now he is being comforted while you are in agony.

The story of the rich man and Lazarus as the church sets it today in the context of the first reading from Amos warns us to behold the signs of God present in our lives and to change our way of living accordingly. The resurrection is not something relegated solely to the end of history. It suffuses all of creation from the beginning. Only in the cross is it fully revealed, but it shines out from every moment. We Christians acknowledge that we have received this good news, as Paul tells Timothy. And we are not to retreat from it.

We believe the action of Christ is constantly leading all things to glory in this present moment. Do we heed these signs? Or do we wait for the great sign as the rich man might have done? If we do not see and appreciate the small signs of God's grace, will not we, like the rich man's brothers, fail to recognize such a great wonder as the resurrection of the dead?

Where do you see God working in your life? Do we take time to acknowledge God's presence in our midst? Do we take seriously our mission to share the good news of our experience of God's grace with others? When we begin sharing the good news, perhaps we might take a clue from the parable and share the little moments in which God coaxes us to holiness. It is hard for someone today to leap from no belief to trust in the resurrection, unexpected as it is. But if we can share our small resurrection experiences, others may come to see their lives touched by similar epiphanies. Then led by their own experiences of God, they might also come to believe in the resurrection of the dead—the final meaning of our existence.

Twenty-Seventh Sunday of the Year

CYCLE A

Isaiah 5:1–7 The vineyard of the Lord God of hosts is the house of Israel.

Philippians 4:6–9 The God of peace be with you.

Matthew 21:33–43 He leased his vineyard to other farmers.

It is comforting to look at our relationship with God as something that cannot be taken from us. And this is true, but the first and gospel readings remind us that our affiliation is just that—"a relationship," a covenant. It must be continuously affirmed and engaged upon. The vineyard does not respond to the master's care and concern. In Jesus' parable, the tenants do not respond as they should even when he sends his son. Our covenant with God is a living collaboration. In it we are to grow and be transformed. We are to become more like God. If we take it for granted or ignore it, how do we expect the Lord to act? We are ignoring God. We are not fulfilling what we have accepted by joining in the covenant.

So we might expect times of hardship and reversal. But notice in the gospel what these hard times are really for. They are not for punishment. They are given to us so that we might wake up and behold the marvels of God. It is very easy to become complacent. But think of it: God has invited us to join in God's work. And that effort continues in our lives and our world. We must be alert to God's signs in our lives. The vineyard and the workers have experienced many effects of God in their lives but they ignored them, explained them away, or turned them to their own ends.

In our sharing of the gospel, how alert are we to what God is saying? Do we truly listen, or do we hear only what we want to hear? When things go wrong, do we use this as an opportunity to discover God's will? Do we use adversity to ascertain for ourselves the marvel that God seeks to disclose?

CYCLE B

Genesis 2:18–24 They were two in one flesh.

Hebrews 2:9–11 He who sanctifies and those who are sanctified have one origin.

Mark 10:2–16 What God has joined together, we must not divide.

The first reading and the gospel focus upon marriage. Jumping off from these readings, marriage often symbolizes our relationship to God. The prophets frequently compare God's love for Israel to marriage. Saint Paul extends the image when he talks of Christ's love for the church.

Let us consider Christian marriage as a sign of good news. We live in a culture where divorce is common, abortion an option, and many women and children are abused. Most of us are married; how can our commitment to

Christian marriage be a sign to others of our loving and faithful God? Every sacrament is not only an encounter with the saving Christ for the people who receive it, but in turn makes those receiving the sacrament a sign of Christ to the world at large.

How might we Christian couples show our culture the joys of faithful love? How might we better show the happiness and fulfillment to be found in a stable and loving family? How can we as a Christian community provide hope and help to married people to remain faithful to their vows and to their original love, which was a live experience of God?

Certainly we can call people to the realization that the love they encounter in a committed relationship is an apprehension of God. Such love is freely given, faithful, and usually fruitful of life. The God we seek to share in evangelization is not some far-off, unattainable experience but is found at the very center of human life—in the loving relationship of one to another.

CYCLE C

Habakkuk 1:2–3; 2:2–4 The just will live by faithfulness.

2 Timothy 1:6–8, 13–14 Never be ashamed of witnessing the Lord.

Luke 17:5–10 If you had faith!

Paul counsels Timothy not to be timid or ashamed of his mission to preach the gospel. We might feel that same timidity or fear as we try on the role of evangelists. First of all, we often feel we are not sufficiently prepared. Yet hopefully we are qualified enough to live out our faith in our lives. That experience is all we really need in order to share the good news. Evangelization is not about expounding the intricacies of the catechism. It is about making people feel welcome and accepted, about joining in the struggles for justice for all people, about being a peacemaker in times of crisis. Such is our call from baptism onward.

Yes, as Jesus says, we do not have much faith, but our faith will increase if we are willing to follow through on our commitment to gospel values. We are not called to some extraordinary life. Missionaries need not be full-time professionals. Every one of us is by baptism a servant of the Lord: it is the Lord's work that we as a church, a parish, families, and individuals need to be about.

Twenty-Eighth Sunday of the Year

CYCLE A

Isaiah 25:6–10 The Lord will prepare a feast and will wipe away the tears from every cheek.

Philippians 4:12–14, 19–20 I am able to do all things in him who strengthens me.

Matthew 22:1–14 Whomsoever you find invite to the wedding.

Isaiah offers a wonderful image of our hope—the gathering of all peoples at the great feast on the Lord's mountain. As we gather together for the Eucharist, we foreshadow this great moment. The bread and wine represent the abundance of food that will be there. And we embody all of the Earth's peoples who will then be present. Seen in this light, the Eucharist is a sign of what God is about. It is a foretaste of that great day. The food we share today is but a foretaste of the heavenly food; the community we experience now but a hint of that great populace.

Let us keep this vision in mind as we celebrate together. We do so not only for ourselves, but on behalf of all who will someday join us around that holy mountain. If we allow this image to guide our participation, it can remind us in our ordinary lives of God's hope and aid us in furthering the realization of that hope by sharing this vision of unity and fullness with the people we meet.

CYCLE B

Wisdom 7:7–11 In comparison to wisdom, I hold riches as nothing.

Hebrews 4:12–13 The word of God discerns the thoughts and intentions of the heart.

Mark 10:17–30 Go and sell whatever you have and come follow me.

Truth and wisdom are not easily found in our world. And when we do discover wisdom, we find repeatedly that it challenges us. It is not easy to live up to the truth. The demands are great. Time and again, the world hears Christians eager to proclaim the truth. We speak out on issues where our voice differs from commonly held opinions.

But it follows that, when we offer the wisdom we have been given by God, we also speak of God's power that enables us to conform to truth. And even more than God's power, we encounter God's mercy upon us and upon all people. God does not condemn us for failing to live up to truth and wisdom. Rather, God's mercy makes all things finally possible. This hope in God forms the crux of the good news we share with the world. Without hope in God's mercy, truth is too harsh and too much for us.

CYCLE C

2 Kings 5:14–17 He returned to Naaman and acknowledged the Lord to this man of God.

2 Timothy 2:8–13 If we hold firm, we shall reign with Christ.

Luke 17:11–19 It seems that no one has returned to give thanks to God except this stranger.

The story of the ten lepers contrasted with the story of Naaman alludes to the importance of thanksgiving in our lives. Naaman realized where the power of healing came from. He was not an Israelite; rather, he was an enemy soldier. Yet he recognized the God who healed him and went to Elijah to offer presents. When Elijah refuses, Naaman asks for some earth to take with him so that he might properly worship God in a foreign land. He has changed his life because of what happened to him.

Yet in the gospel, nine of the ten lepers do not return to Jesus to give thanks. What happened to them? Did they really experience healing? Did they take it for granted? They were all Israelites except the one who returned.

Do we take forgiveness and healing for granted? Do we still realize what precious gifts healing and forgiveness are? Are we still aware how holy and wonderful are the graces we get from forgiveness and healing? What do we do to make our community a sign of God's healing and forgiveness? How do we reach out to the foreigner, whether that person be poor, an immigrant, or in some other way exiled from the community?

Our reconciliation of such people would be a powerful sign of Jesus' power in our midst. The world expects the church to act as it does. How marvelous when she acts in accord with God rather than the world, when she forgives rather than condemns, when she heals rather than hurts! Such signs, which could be taken for granted, will be seen by the Naamans of our time and may well move them to join us in thanksgiving.

Twenty-Ninth Sunday of the Year

CYCLE A

Isaiah 45:1, 4–6 I have taken the hand of Cyrus to subdue nations before his countenance.

1 Thessalonians 1:1–5 We are mindful of your faith, hope, and love.

Matthew 22:15–21 Give to Caesar the things that belong to Caesar, and to God the things that are God's.

Paul speaks of the hidden dynamics of evangelization. He tells the Thessalonians they were chosen not by Paul's preaching but rather through the power of God that rode upon his words. As evangelists, we are vehicles of God's grace and power. Success does not depend upon us. We are not to congratulate ourselves when it is present or tear ourselves down when it is not. Our role is to be but the means for the conveyance of God's grace. To do so we must be careful, we must prepare, and we must do our best.

But let us also step back. Let us allow room for God; for God plants the seed and causes it to germinate. Much of what we do in announcing the good news depends upon knowing when to get out of the way, so that God's grace can work. A good way to cultivate this practice is to pray right before we undertake any evangelization. In doing so we acknowledge that this is God's work. We give thanks that we have been invited to share in it. And we ask that the power of God be in our words and actions.

CYCLE B

Isaiah 53:10–11 If he offers his life in atonement, he shall see his heirs and have a long life.

Hebrews 4:14–16 Let us be confident in approaching the throne of grace.

Mark 10:35–45 The Son of Man came to give his life as a ransom for many.

The servant is a key image in the first reading and in the gospel. Jesus selects this image as a prime metaphor for Christian life. First of all, he himself models the true servant. He does not act towards his disciples or toward us as other teachers do. Instead he serves us. He cares for us. He goes so far on the last day of his life as to wash his followers' feet.

As disciples of Jesus, we are encouraged to imitate him rather than the rest of the world in its chase after power and dominance. He asks us to be servants to our brothers and sisters. As a community, our church is called to be of service to others. How are we a sign of service in our community? Do we spend our money to help others? Do we consider ourselves called to be of service to our local community? How can we demonstrate to our neighbors that we are a community in service to others?

CYCLE C

Exodus 17:8–13 As long as Moses kept his arms raised, Israel had the advantage.

2 Timothy 3:14–4:2 This is how the child of God becomes equipped and ready for every good work.

Luke 18:1–8 God will see those who cry out vindicated.

The first and gospel readings today speak of patience and perseverance. We are on a long journey. There are plenty of excuses to lose hope. Yet Jesus asks us to have faith. He employs a very down-to-earth and human incident to drive home his point. Consider the pushy widow. She did not have a hope of finding justice from this complacent and self-righteous judge. But that does not stop her or cause her to give up. She keeps pestering him. She will not go away. Finally she wears the judge down. He does not give her justice because he wants to; he does it to get rid of her.

Now if this is the way of a bad judge, what do you think of God, Jesus asks us. Our response should be a huge sigh of relief. Is God as bad as this judge? No, yet the widow was finally vindicated. So why should we lose hope? It is not up to us to bring justice to the world, to gather all into the church family. We are simply here to do our small part. Indeed that is all we are asked to do—all that we can do. And we trust that our small contribution will aid God's plan for reconciliation and the unity of all creation—in God's time.

Thirtieth Sunday of the Year

CYCLE A

Exodus 22:20–26 If you are harsh with the widow or the orphan, my anger will rage against you.

1 Thessalonians 1:5–10 You turned away from idols to serve God and to await his Son.

Matthew 22:34–40 You shall love the Lord your God and your neighbor as yourself.

The second reading shows the primary means of evangelization: modeling. Paul provides a model for the faith when he lives among the Thessalonians. They in turn become examples of the faith for the people of Macedonia and Achaia. Evangelization is not something we preach or do: it is the way we live. And our ultimate model is God.

We find a marvelous description of God's way in the first reading. The Israelites are reminded to be hospitable to the stranger, look out for the widows and orphans, and not place any more burdens upon the poor. Rather they should ease the burdens of the poor. We might bear these words in mind as we go about our civic duties. Do we vote only for ourselves, or do we vote in such a way that keeps in mind the poor and the impact of legislation upon them? What are the consequences of our actions upon those already suffering affliction, oppression, and poverty?

God acts this way out of God's infinite compassion. And we who have experienced that compassion are invited to imitate it and show it in turn to those we meet. At its core our tradition simply asks us to become like God. We are to love God, who has created and sustains us out of love. And we are to act in the same way toward our neighbor.

CYCLE B

Jeremiah 31:7–9 I shall lead them back in mercy—both the blind and the lame.

Hebrews 5:1–6 You are a priest forever according to the order of Melchizedek.

Mark 10:46–52 Master, grant that I may see.

One of the heartbreaks of being physically impaired is the isolation that society often visits upon the person. Those who are not whole in body make the rest of us uncomfortable. They remind us of what could happen to us. Or they make us feel guilty. But for whatever reason, society often shuns the disabled.

However, the kingdom of God is for all people; the blind, lame, and deaf are especially acknowledged and included in the kingdom, as Jeremiah points out. In the gospel we see the people trying to keep Bartimaeus from Jesus. They want to exclude him from Jesus' company, but Jesus hears Bartimaeus and reaches out to him in healing.

As a Christian community, in the name of Jesus we also reach out to include all people. We may take steps to make our church and our community accessible to those in wheelchairs. We may have a person sign our services for those who are deaf. The kingdom of God is for all people, not just the fit. We follow Jesus when we show no discrimination in our treatment of people and when we provide opportunity for all people in whatever way challenged to feel at home in our church and in society at large.

CYCLE C

Sirach 35:12–14, 16–18 The prayer of the humble one will penetrate the heavens.

2 Timothy 4:6–8, 16–18 All that remains is the crown of righteousness reserved for me.

Luke 18:8–14 The publican returned home justified, the pharisee did not.

The first and gospel readings today speak of God's impartiality. We are all loved and accepted equally. But it is difficult to see equality in our world. It is even hard to see it in our church. It is easy for us to see ourselves as the saved and others in need of us. But when we do so we turn into the Pharisee of the parable. God sees no difference between these two men. Both are sinners; both are the focus of God's mercy and forgiveness. So it is with us.

We are all, Christian and non-Christian alike, in the same position. We are all of us sinners; and we are all of us saved through the cross of Christ. As Christians we are aware of that truth: we celebrate it and allow it to transform our lives. But we are still sinners. And non-Christians are just as beloved by God as we are. Our mission is to share the good news of that love we have experienced and have recognized as Jesus Christ.

Thirty-First Sunday of the Year

CYCLE A

Malachi 1:14–2:2, 8–10 You have strayed from the way, you have caused many to stumble by your teaching.

1 Thessalonians 2:7–9,13 We were eager to hand over to you not only the good news but our lives as well.

Matthew 23:1–12 They do not practice what they preach.

In today's epistle, Paul gives appropriate advice for the would-be evangelizer. First he speaks of the tenderness of the ministry—he acts like a nursing mother caring for her infant. Our message is essentially one of God's overwhelming love. We speak of God's kindness and concern reaching out to us again and again throughout Israel's history and finally in Jesus. Our message must reflect and communicate that love—not just speak of it. And we must first love those to whom we bring the good news, so that as Paul says, we are willing to share our very lives with them. Evangelization is not some job that occupies us for a certain amount of time; it is a way of living that we seek to practice constantly. And this lifestyle calls us to be a part of the community with whom we wish to share the good news.

Finally, Paul speaks of his concern that he not be a burden to the community he is evangelizing. He provides for himself rather than seeking support from them. Today such a situation is unlikely, but the principle still remains valid. Does our message impose a burden on the people with whom we wish to share the gospel? Is it a message of hope that lightens our life, or is it a word that places added burdens upon people? Being human, we are tempted to convert through force or fear. But to do so betrays the good news we bear.

CYCLE B

Deuteronomy 6:2–6 Hear, Israel, you shall love the Lord with all your heart.

Hebrews 7:23–28 This one, because he remains forever, has an eternal priesthood.

Mark 12:28–34 This is the first commandment, and the second is similar to it.

It is very easy in our faith to lose sight of the forest for the trees. What is really central to our faith, and what is simply a matter of time or culture? The first reading and today's gospel bring us back to the core of our faith life. We are called to love God and to love one another as ourselves. If we can show the world our love of God and of one another, we become a sign to the world of God's care and concern for all.

Jesus is both the sign of God's love for us and the inviting of our own love toward God. In his life he continually reveals God's love and concern for all. In the outpouring of his life on the cross, he demonstrates the extent to which God's love is willing to go out to us. Christians respond to this love by loving and being grateful to God in return. And we endeavor to act godlike ourselves through our love for our neighbor.

All we have to offer the world is Jesus: his life, his stories, the stories about him. We call this gift good news—gospel. In our lives we act lovingly because we have experienced loving action toward us. We hope that others may come to see such love in our lives and may also be drawn into the source of that love which is God as we experience the divine in Jesus.

CYCLE C

Wisdom 11:22–12:1 You have mercy on all things because you love everything that exists.

2 Thessalonians 1:11–2:2 The name of our Lord Jesus Christ will be glorified in you and you in him.

Luke 19:1–10 The Son of Man came to seek and to find that which was lost.

The reading from Wisdom provides a wonderful meditation upon the goodness of God and creation. There is nothing created that God does not love and cherish. Yet it is human nature to want to draw lines and say what is good and what is not, who is acceptable and who is not. Perhaps the greatest message we have today is to proclaim God's love for all creation over and over.

If we become aware of God's love for all creation, we must then refine our own attitude toward nature and her many creatures. The gospel story of Zacchaeus takes God's love for all into the human sphere. His neighbors do not find Zacchaeus a very lovable person. After all, he is cooperating with the oppressor and living off the misery of his townsfolk. Who could blame them for ostracizing him?

Yet Jesus invites himself into Zacchaeus' house and asks hospitality of him. Jesus will not exclude him, avoid him, or judge him. Instead he desires to dine with him. In this culture, dining is an intimate act shared only with friends and family.

By first reaching out to Zacchaeus, Jesus enables him to respond in kind. In our own evangelization, we must continually strive to reach out to those ignored or excluded by others. These people are just as beloved of God, just as valuable and cherished by God as are the powerful, generous, or talented.

Thirty-Second Sunday of the Year

CYCLE A

Wisdom 6:12–16 Wisdom is found by those who look for it.

1 Thessalonians 4:13–17 Those who died as Christians, God will bring to life with Jesus.

Matthew 25:1–13 Look, the bridegroom comes. Go out to meet him.

The second reading invites us to consider a special group of people for evangelization: those who are afraid of death or nearing death. Our culture denies death and even old age. We speak of it in euphemisms: Mother passed away. We hide our old people away in homes and often neglect them there.

For the Christian, death is no enemy but rather a friend. Saint Francis even called her "sister." Death is not the end or annihilation but a joyful passing over into a new life with the One we love. Many of our neighbors are afraid of death. How can we live the good news so that they come to see death as a friend? Certainly those of us who are ill and dying are especially chosen for this particular ministry. It is easy to talk of death and eternal life when we are not under its shadow. But when we are close to death what power to share the gospel we have if we can live in such a way that people witness our acceptance of death and our desire to be with the Lord.

CYCLE B

1 Kings 17:10–16 The widow made a little scone from her flour meal and brought it to Elijah.

Hebrews 9:24–28 Christ offered himself only once to take the faults of many on himself.

Mark 12:38–44 This poor widow has put more in than all who contributed.

When Catholics think about evangelization, we are likely to find ourselves in the position of the two women in today's readings. We do not feel we have enough faith to be able to share it with others. We have memories of all the different dogmas and rules that we learned in catechism, and we do not feel on top of the catechism. We may see ourselves as simply hanging on to the barque of Peter. We certainly do not feel ourselves capable of navigating or steering it.

These readings reassure us. We are asked to give of what we have, and God will take care of us. Certainly the widow in the gospel does not give nearly as much as the rich people. Yet Jesus singles her out for praise because she has given from her need.

When we find ourselves in situations where we do not think we have much to offer, let us remember this story. For example, when someone is grieving a death, especially the death of a young person, we may find ourselves without any words of explanation. Why did this happen? Why does God allow such tragedy? No one can explain why. But we can be one with the grieving in their sorrow. When we share their grief we have compassion—we "stand with" them in their pain. We can share our hope that all is in God's hands. We might speak of our trust in a God who has partaken in our own sorrow through his crucifixion.

We are not explaining things, making everything right. We are speaking from our own need. We stand with our friends in their sorrow and share our resources with them: our own feeble faith. We do so not to convert them, but to be with them, just as God has revealed in Jesus that God is with us at all times.

CYCLE C

2 Maccabees 7:1–2, 9–14 The king of the world will receive us into life eternal at the resurrection.

2 Thessalonians 2:16–3:5 May the Lord strengthen you in everything good that you do or say.

Luke 20:27–38 God is not a God of the dead but of the living.

At the core of Jesus' message lies the gift of eternal life, or resurrection. And this gift is not something to be received after we die or in the future. Jesus invites us to begin living this new richer life now. Once we have a taste of the new life God offers us as a gift, we know we can never go back to the old way of living.

The story of the seven brothers can be read in two ways. From one perspective, we can concentrate upon the cruelty of their martyrdom. They are victims for their faith. But chances are they would interpret what happened to them quite differently. The last brother witnesses to the life that God gives. Once we have tasted that life no other life makes sense. When we evangelize, we have a message about this richer life, but to be effective our evangelization must go beyond words. That richer life is present now within our community, and we must share it with others so that they too may come to know it.

Many people testify that the first time they entered a Catholic church they felt a presence, something that made them feel at peace and happy. They often cannot explain it, but they say that once they felt it they kept coming back and finally had to claim it for themselves. This is the treasure God has entrusted to us—this treasure of life everlasting. How can we enable more of our neighbors to experience this treasure with us? We do not need to convince them of the gospel. Let them experience the new life, and they will be hooked.

Thirty-Third Sunday of the Year

CYCLE A

Proverbs 31:10–13, 19–20, 30–31 Give her a share in what she has worked for.

1 Thessalonians 5:1–6 The day of the Lord is going to come like a thief in the night.

Matthew 25:14–30 Because you have been faithful over a few things, enter into the joy of the Lord.

We can draw two instructions about evangelization from today's scriptures. Paul exhorts the Thessalonians to be watchful and awake. The natural state of humanity is spiritual sleep. We can see this very clearly in the gospels—almost anytime something truly important is happening the disciples are asleep or want to go to sleep:

on the mount of Transfiguration, in the garden of Gethsemane, at the resurrection.

The gospel is like a spiritual alarm clock that awakens us to see, enjoy, and rejoice in God's magnificent creation and the life we have been given. Here is a twofold ministry for evangelizers: First, we must keep ourselves awake to the moment. How is God appearing in our lives and our world this minute? With what opportunities does God present us to share the gospel right now?

Second, our message itself is a call to wake up. A wonderful life is unfolding in an awesome creation. Let us savor it to the fullest and give thanks for the gift. Of course, this good news is directed at ourselves as much as to those with whom we wish to share the gospel.

The gospel reading emphasizes seizing the opportunity. Fear drives our world. It is easy to identify with the third individual in the parable. In our ministry of evangelization, we might question whether our faith is sufficient or strong enough. What if we make mistakes? What if our ministry turns people off to us and to the message we carry? What if we are not listened to? We may be tempted to bury this ministry in the ground to keep it and ourselves safe.

But notice the way the world of the story works: two people gamble and their risks are abundantly rewarded. If reality truly works this way rather than the way we and the third character fear it does, we are fools if we do not take every chance.

As Christians what do we really have to lose? No one and nothing can separate us from Christ. In the light of that assurance, any other fear pales into insignificance. We have been entrusted with a treasure—our faith. The only way we can use the gift wrongly is not to use it at all.

CYCLE B

Daniel 12:1–3 When that time comes your own people will be spared.

Hebrews 10:11–14,18 By a single offering he has achieved the eternal perfection of all these who are sanctified.

Mark 13:24–32 He shall gather his elect from the four winds.

Mainstream Christianity has often been wary of these apocalyptic texts. Paul had trouble with the Thessalonians over their interpretation of the end of the world. Although we believe that the world will end, most of us do not think too much about it and are uncomfortable with those who try to link such texts to current events.

Yet the judgment of God is an essential part of Jesus' gospel and of our whole tradition. One of our tasks as evangelists is to point to this divine judgment and explain how it hangs over our world today. While we do not interpret these texts in terms of a time and place (in fact today's gospel tells us we cannot do so), we can point to elements of our modern world that may place us under God's judgment.

How are we using our natural resources? Are we taking care of the world or exploiting it? We need not resort to biblical texts to awaken us to the consequences of our neglect. We live in troubled times: a season of plague, famine, destruction. The gospel recognizes these afflictions and holds out a message of hope in spite of them. God is still Lord of history and desires us to turn to God and to align ourselves with God's purpose. Such is the good news we are given to share with our neighbors.

CYCLE C

Malachi 3:19–20 The sun of righteousness will shine on you.

2 Thessalonians 3:7–12 If anyone refuses to work then do not let them eat.

Luke 21:5–19 Your endurance will win you your life.

Today's readings can be seen in at least two ways. First, we can use them as warnings. Watch out, the end is coming and it's going to be bad. A lot of Christians delight in the worsening world situation. But Catholics do not scorn the world. We are sent by God to be in the world and be leaven to the world.

Being a follower of Jesus is bound to lead us up against the world. We may be doing our best, but the world seems to be getting worse and worse. So we might see today's readings not as a warning but as a description of how bad things can get. Yet this situation provides no reason to despair. God is still God and is still caring and loving of creation. In spite of the present darkness, if we keep faith there will be a new dawn of healing and justice.

It is not up to us to save the world, but to be faithful to our mission to speak and live good news. As long as we witness to what we know of our loving God, we can rest assured that in the end "not a hair of your head will perish." Such good news comforts us and all our world in our times of crisis. We and our community need to reassure ourselves frequently with this good news.

Last Sunday of the Year—
Christ the King

CYCLE A

Ezekiel 34:11–12, 15–17 You, my flock, I judge between sheep and sheep, between rams and he-goats.

1 Corinthians 15:20–26, 28 He will hand over the kingdom to God the Father, so that God may be all in all.

Matthew 25:31–46 He will sit upon his seat of glory and he will separate them one from another.

The gospel of the Last Judgment once more drives home the point that true evangelization comes through living, not through preaching or thinking. When have we neglected you, Lord? Whenever we fail to see another human being, especially another in need and misery, as Jesus himself, we betray the gospel and the message entrusted us. It is easy to talk. It is often fun to debate and argue. It can be intoxicating to theologize. And all of these activities have genuine value.

However, our real calling, our real mission in carrying the gospel, is to love our neighbor as we love God and to act accordingly. We know that God has loved us. We have experienced that love reaching out to nourish, heal, clothe, and visit us. In whatever way we can reach out to our neighbor (and neighbor here includes family, friend, coworker, Catholic brother or sister, and every other human being) in love, we are fulfilling the calling Jesus gives us to preach the gospel.

CYCLE B

Daniel 7:13–14 His sovereignty is eternal.

Revelation 1:5–8 The ruler of the kings of the earth...made us a line of kings, priests to serve his God.

John 18:33–37 You say that I am a king.

While Christians may be tempted to think of Christ the King as the king of all kings and the greatest of kings, such was not Jesus' understanding of monarchy. His is a hidden kingship. He stands before Pilate, the representative of the Roman ruler, without any visible power or authority. Yet when questioned about his kingship, Jesus replies with the simple truth even though it seems wholly out of touch with his current predicament.

We Christians profess that Jesus is our king. But even today his is a hidden kingdom—not of this world. His people are the poor and outcast. He sides with the downtrodden. And indeed his kingship is fully revealed in this gospel passage as he is about to be executed as a common troublemaker. We make Christ our king when we honor his subjects, the poor and defenseless.

We acknowledge his sovereignty over us when we adhere to his vision and values in the face of competing loyalties. We acclaim Christ king when we show respect for all life—unborn, mentally and physically challenged, the old and feeble, and even criminal. We make him our king when we model our lives after his and assume the role of servant rather than ruler.

When we truly understand and present to the world the way in which Jesus is king, he ceases to compete with other rulers and powers. It is not a case of my king can beat your king. No, when we understand the monarchy of

Jesus we come to see what a real king is, and we realize there is no other like him.

CYCLE C

2 Samuel 5:1–3 They anointed David king of Israel.

Colossians 1:12–20 God has taken us into the kingdom of the beloved Son.

Luke 23:35–43 Lord, remember me when you come into your kingdom.

Today's second reading speaks of Christ at the center of all creation. He is the image in which all is created. He is the essence of everything that is. If this is so, then all is truly in Christ. Nothing is unloved; nothing is of less value than Christ.

The problem is that people, even Christians, are blind to this truth. We think of Christ as different from ourselves. We are sinners; Christ is not. Yes, we are sinners, but in sinning we go against our very nature, which is Christ. That is why we become miserable. We are acting as someone we are not. We are deceiving ourselves and others as well.

If Christ is the very image in which we are made, then Christ is the very image of everyone who is made and of everything that is created. When we look deeply into another, the Christ in us recognizes the Christ in them. If we were really conscious of this, how could we act hurtfully to anyone or anything? Only when we forget the Christ within us and within others can we fall into acting selfishly or pridefully, wanting to gain more for ourselves even if it means depriving others.

Today's feast enlarges upon this idea. We call Christ "the King." And perhaps we even treat him as a king. And we think of ourselves as his subjects. Christians have even gone to war for this king of peace. But when Jesus is called a king the very meaning of the word is called into question. Here is a king with no earthly power, no earthly realm. Here is a king of beggars who is himself a beggar. Here is a king who is a servant to the lowest person in his kingdom. Here is a king who gives himself as a gift to his subjects rather than collecting gifts and tributes from his subjects as any natural king would do.

When we come to see the royalty of the Christ in Jesus he does not acknowledge it and accept our tribute. As he says to the thief, "Today you will be with me in Paradise." He takes us into his kingship. He acknowledged the same royalty in us. We could perform no greater work of evangelization in our ordinary lives than we do by acknowledging in everyone and everything we encounter the same Christ that is at the very center of our own being. To do so would change all.

6

Other Solemnities

June 29—Feast of Saints Peter and Paul

Acts of the Apostles 12:1–11 Now I know it is indeed true: the Lord has saved me from the power of Herod.

2 Timothy 4:6–8, 17–18 All that remains now is the crown of righteousness.

Matthew 16:13–19 You are Peter; and I will give you the keys of the Kingdom of heaven.

The fact that we are Catholic Christians is an essential part of our evangelization message. We belong to a great company of witnesses stretching back through the ages to the first Christians. Among those witnesses, Peter and Paul share a special place. Like many, they are martyrs for the faith. The word martyr means "witness." Peter, who had denied Jesus during his Passion, goes so far as to ask that he be crucified upside-down. What a tremendous impression that action makes upon us even today. That he would so honor his Lord as to count himself not good enough to share his fate: the disciple unworthy a proper crucifixion.

Paul's fervor shows the model evangelist. He carried the message of Jesus throughout most of his world. Both he and Peter died far from home, in the capital city of their day—Rome. Chances are that our mission will not carry us so far from our homes. However, are we willing, like Peter and Paul, to give the Spirit the chance to lead us where the Spirit wants? It might not be far in terms of geography, but it could be far in other ways.

August 6—
Feast of Transfiguration

Daniel 7:9–10, 13–14 His raiment was as white as snow.
2 Peter 1:16–19 We heard this voice from out of heaven.
Gospel:

A: Matthew 17:1–9 His face was shining like the sun.

B: Mark 9:2–10 This is my Son, my beloved.

C: Luke 9:29–36 As he was praying his face was transformed.

Today's feast is concerned with God's glory. Peter, James, and John are witnesses to that glory on the mountain of Transfiguration. Let us first ask ourselves how we have experienced the glory of God. In order for us to be effective evangelists we must first have been witness to the glory of God in our lives. How have we seen it? How have we seen it in our community? What actions in this church show forth God's light? How do we celebrate? How does our music, our visual arts, our liturgy shine with that light? What groups and people within our church shine with this light as they serve the poor, minister to the sick, welcome the homeless, educate children? Who is on fire, enlightened, by their faith so we can see it in their faces? This is how we come to share the disciples' experience.

The gospel ends by saying that they kept silent about this and told no one. At first this might seem quite contrary to the idea that we must proclaim the good news. But this gospel is describing the process by which evangelists are made. Once they have seen the glory, they then keep silent for a time. But not forever. After Easter, Jesus sends them out to shout the good news.

There is a time of incubation after we have seen the glory. We keep it within our hearts and allow its light to enlighten us, change us, deepen our insight.

In the Gospels, we usually think of Mary doing this—pondering all things in her heart. But we are all called to take time to reflect and allow the light to work within us. We must be transformed before we are ready to proclaim the good news. Knowing when to be silent and when it is time to proclaim belongs to the gift of wisdom from the Holy Spirit.

August 15—Assumption of the Blessed Virgin Mary

Revelation 11:19; 12:1–6, 10 I saw a woman clothed with the sun and with the moon beneath her feet.

1 Corinthians 15:20–26 As members of Christ all people will be raised. Christ first, and after him all who belong to him.

Luke 1:39–56 God who is mighty has done great things for me; God has exalted the humble.

Today's feast is in a sense the conclusion of the gospel story if we read the gospel as it is proclaimed through culture rather than simply the written gospels. Beneath the incidents of the gospel, we can trace a deeper story—an eternal story—a love story.

And how does a love story go? We all know it: boy meets girl, girl and boy fall in love, boy loses girl, boy and girl become reunited and live happily ever after. Even if the lovers die, they die together in their love; something in that pattern is deeply satisfying to all human beings.

In Jesus, God takes up that pattern of things which God implanted from the beginning in human consciousness and God here gives it concrete shape. We are the beloved. We have lost our way, but we will one day be reunited with God in the kingdom. Mary is a foretaste of what will happen on the last day to all creation. All will be gathered up into God's embrace. Such is the hope that this feast inspires within us.

Right now it is still a hopeful vision. The creation is not in harmony. Injustice and evil are quite present among us. Like Mary in today's gospel, this is our concern as Christians. We look and wait for the day when the mighty will be tumbled and the low raised up, the hungry will be filled with good foods, and we servants of the Lord will be upheld in front of the world. How do we as individuals and community embody these signs in our world? Do people see in us a place where the hungry are fed, where everyone shares the same status as children of God? How can we make these signs more visible to our neighbors and to the world?

November 1—Feast of All Saints

Revelation 7:2–4, 9–14 I saw an immense crowd, beyond hope of counting, of people from every nation, race, tribe and language.

1 John 3:1–3 We shall see God as God really is.

Matthew 5:1–12 Rejoice and be glad for your reward will be great in heaven.

While Catholics today regard this feast as a celebration of the canonical saints, in the earliest church all members were saints, since all were called to a life of sanctity. A saint is a person who is united with God, as we see in the first reading. John reminds us that we are children of God. But we are becoming something more. We are becoming like Christ. We are imbued with his light; our work as disciples is to be transformed by that light. The canonical saints suffered this transformation, and they in turn became beacons of light who led people to Jesus.

In the Beatitudes Jesus offers a number of paths to real happiness (union with God). These provide clues as to how we might undergo further conversion—how we might be "divinized" as our Orthodox brothers and sisters speak of this journey. By committing ourselves and our community to this ongoing pilgrimage of sanctification (as the Western Church likes to call it), we will provide for all people beacons that will lead them to our source and our light—Jesus Christ.

December 8—Immaculate Conception

Genesis 3:9–15, 20 I will place enmity between your seed and the seed of the woman.

Ephesians 1:3–4, 11–12 God chose us in Christ before the foundation of the world.

Luke 1:26–38 Rejoice, favored one, the Lord is with you.

This feast tells us that there are no limits upon God's saving power. Mary was preserved from original sin through the power of the cross even before Jesus was born. In the second reading, Paul tells us how God has chosen us before the world began. That God chose us does not imply that God rejected others. We have the freedom to reject the divine love. But it is hoped that each person will, like Mary, freely assent to God's offer.

Like Mary, we too have received a message. The word angel in Greek means a message or the Word of God. And like Mary we have said "Yes" to that Word. How do we give birth to the Word? How do we bring the Word we have heard into our family, our neighborhood, our community, our world?

The Immaculate Conception is about new beginnings. We celebrate a woman whom God protected from sin so that she might give birth to the savior. This is our national feast day. And we Americans also believe in new beginnings. Our ancestors came here from elsewhere so that they might begin again. That day of American innocence is now far off. But God constantly offers us and all people the chance to begin again anew: in baptism and reconciliation. The offer of forgiveness is never taken away.

How can we, both individuals and community, alert people to the possibility of new beginnings as they come to know the gospel? Are we a church that is willing to make mistakes and sins, acknowledge them, and receive the forgiveness and grace to move on? Or are we unwilling to accept anything less than perfection in ourselves and others? Mary's sinlessness is not of her own doing. She is preserved by God and by Jesus Christ. We are in the same position, although we have indeed truly sinned. Yet that sin never forfeits the gift of forgiveness.

POSTSCRIPT

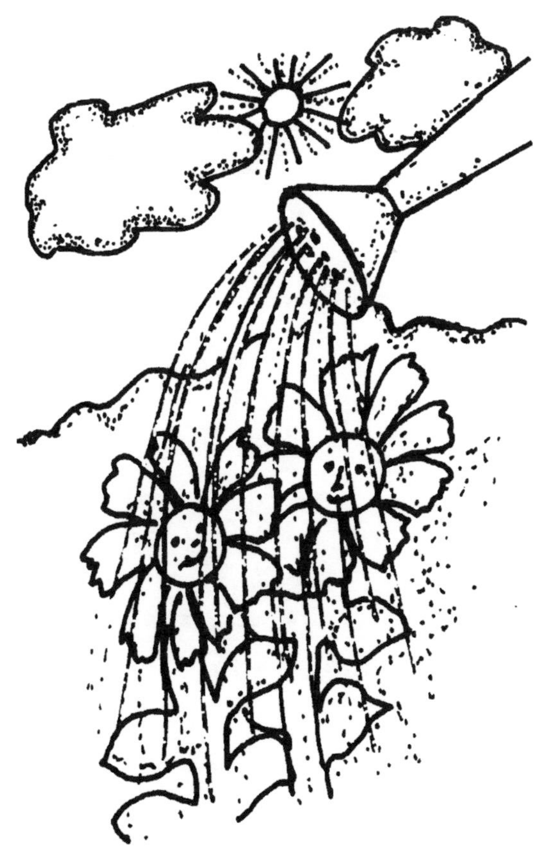

If you have worked through a number of these readings to see them in an evangelizing light, you have come to see that evangelization is the proper key to use with all scripture. Of course, not every homily need focus exclusively or even glancingly on evangelization. But we should read scripture aware that most of it was written from an evangelizing perspective. This is certainly true of both the gospels and the epistles. Paul writes because he is trying to convert or evangelize more deeply the congregations he founded. The gospel writers write both to deepen the faith of their communities and to convince others of the trustworthiness of the gospel. When we lose sight of this implicit dimension of Christian scripture, we dull the message. No one would write for the already converted. What is the need?

And it should be obvious as well that evangelization is not only an ongoing dimension of our Christian mission, but that we grow and change as we come to be evangelized more deeply. Three years from now, our community will be different in its understanding of the faith. So our message will need to change, to call us ever more deeply into the evangelizing mission. What will that demand? How will we cope with the task?

We cannot and should not attempt to answer such questions. We are every one of us upon a journey of faith. We cannot anticipate the problems of tomorrow nor the means of solving them. But we can come to a deeper level of trust that God will provide and that our ministry of evangelization will grow. In doing so, it will transform ourselves and our communities. We cannot know what words we shall need then. The Word of God is a living word and therefore a present word. Let us trust that tomorrow's word will be given us when we need it.

And finally, although this book has been mostly about words, let us not forget that evangelization is not confined nor even best exemplified by words. Keep foremost in mind the exhortation of Saint Francis of Assisi to his disciples: "Evangelize in everything you do." And if necessary even do it through words. Churches, structures, and, above all, actions all speak louder than any preaching. So let our preaching be in the service of transforming the many ways in which others encounter us and come to know us. We have a great message. It has been entrusted to us by someone who knows all our faults and weaknesses. Let us take comfort in the fact that God knows exactly what God is doing. We are the earthen vessels that carry such a treasure.